Higher Laws from Beyond the Veil

Insights about the true nature of God, prayer and the laws that govern all interactions on earth.

By Marcus Deius

MarcusDeius.com

ISBN: 1-948689-00-6
ISBN-13: 978-1-948689-00-7

Contents

Preface

The Light

I finally understood the native language of the country in which I was serving a mission. The only problem was I found myself hovering over a lifeless body in the middle of an operating room. Though they did not teach medical vocabulary in the Missionary Training Center, I had gathered that I was going in for open chest surgery, and they were debating which of three methods they were going to use to open my chest. In a flurry of commands, the doctor barked out orders to do this and that; all were frantically trying to bring this skinny and very pale person "back." This person was an American - and even looked sort of like me, but it did not make sense as I tried to explain to the surgeon, I was fine.

It was almost comical because I was better than fine. I felt perfect. In every conceivable way, I was in complete peace. However, I began losing focus due to the drama in the operating room. I was suddenly jolted, and, with unimaginable speed, I left the operating room and hospital. The rate was so incredible; it was something I still can't describe. Like a slingshot and in a flash of trans-dimensional movement, I was transported to a place of glorious energy or light. It was exhilarating! I was surrounded by a loving warmth that increased into a sublime ecstasy of indescribable and outrageous bliss. I directed my attention to the source, and I became engulfed in an unfathomable, benevolent, virtuous, overwhelmingly powerful, perfect, unconditional love. It was radiating from a being that I will call: The Light. I cannot call this being mere "God" because He was so much more and so different from what I had been taught. This Being was made of all-knowing, blinding power, yet above all else, was permeating all-encompassing love.

When I say "all-knowing," I mean it. He knew everything about me, as my entire 20 years of life was suddenly before us. The overwhelming, unconditional love was apparent as we were completely aware of every single major or minor act I had ever done. The ripples from these actions and every single fickle, immature, mean, angry, hurtful, or embarrassing thing I had done was fully known to both of us. I felt so unaware of wasting so much of my life in these feelings because, with just a hint of this new, broader, and eternal perspective, it was just such a squandering of so many of life's moments. Yet, while I felt ashamed, the feeling just melted away because The Light radiated nothing but perfect love, zero condemnation, and complete understanding. Why The Light was not angry, upset, or even disappointed filled me with questions, and with that, the most significant answers started to flow unto me as fast as the questions formed. I had a sense that there was nothing I could not know when I was with the Light.

This was just the beginning of the most profound lesson of my lifetime, in which if I live a million more lifetimes, I will never have learned even a fraction of that which I knew in those moments of being with The Light.

I know Joseph Smith Jr. pronounced that one cannot have a testimony about God unless he or she has a correct understanding of the true nature of God.[1] This was entirely true, and yet the being I studied on earth was not the same being with whom I was interacting. He was not a wrathful being, and he could never have been. I understood with absolute perfection that in the mortal plane with mortal minds, nobody has the capacity to fully understand a mere fraction of all that God is. I seemed to be unlimited in that realm, not like my mind on earth. As I relished in connection with infinite wisdom, my mind flooded with lifelong questions in which the answers only parlayed into more questions. And with a sort of

---

[1] King Follett Sermon - April 7, 1844.

heavenly pleasure, the Light somehow assured me that "all will be answered," and my journey began.

I had what I later learned was a Near Death Experience or NDE. Though I can never agree with that term, it was more like 'near visit-to-life-eternal.' There is no such thing as death, nor is death anything to fear but to rejoice. In essence, all that you seek in life will be granted to you in 'death.'

This is not a book about my experience, per se. My experience was my experience; it was for me. I saw and was taught perfectly and saw countless examples to every query that flashed across my mind. And then I was told I was to return. I disagreed (strangely enough), for I already was home, but this was not a matter of discussion. The saddest moment of my life was returning to this earthly realm in which I now had little comparable interest.

The first thing I remembered as I came back was the nurses who were trying to fit my body in a bed that was too small for me. My chest felt like it was pummeled with baseball bats. I could not shake the sadness at longer being with The Light. Nothing was more delicious than swimming in that presence. My connection to all true knowledge was fleeting, and I simply did not have the capacity here as when I was with The Light. Panicking, I grasped onto as much knowledge as I could remember. The Light's last fleeting message was to be calm because I would always have access to the essence of the knowledge whenever I needed it, and whatever I looked for, I would find. Then everything went black.

I feel the topics of this book are of paramount importance for many, though they were my questions for me and my life. This book starts with the nature of God and continues about our true relationship with God and how prayer fits into the equation of how and why things happen to each of us. This book is to remind those who are seeking how much more powerful we are to affect our lives and the lives of others. This book is solely about directing you to your own inner direction because inner-direction is the master key to unlocking all there is.

It is difficult to explain a flood of information in a line upon line format. It was as if I was connected to the most extensive library in the universe, and anything I wanted to know, I knew instantly; or rather, thinking of the question uncovered the answers from my memory. But as soon as I returned to my body, I no longer had full access, just fleeting memories. Though I am usually a positive person, this was the saddest time of my life because I just wanted to go back. Though now, when I read the scriptures or see interactions and manifestations in life, I can see the true meaning behind these former mysteries. I can see the efficacy and lack of efficacy in how people think, pray, and live. I see the disturbing fruits of my friends, neighbors, and strangers, of a life not lived in true harmony with God or the Laws. I can no longer sit by and watch. This book is to appease my soul and answer the questions of people who are asking.

Not until after I melted into The Light and experienced infinity did I understand these quotes from Joseph Smith Jr.:

> "Brethren, if I were to tell you all I know of the kingdom of God, I do know that you would rise up and kill me.'[2]

> "If I revealed all that has been made known to me, scarcely a man on this stand would stay with me." "The Prophet Joseph said to me [Brigham Young], about sixteen years ago [at Kirtland], 'If I was to show the Latter-day Saints all the revelations that the Lord has shown unto me, there is scarce a man that would stay with me, they could not bear it.'"[3]

> "Would to God, brethren, I could tell you who I am! Would to God I could tell you WHAT I know! But you would call it blasphemy and...want to take my life!"[4]

There were many more things I saw and learned while with The

---

[2] As recalled by Parley P. Pratt in Millennial Star 55 [Sept. 4 1893]: 585.
[3] Millennial Star 17 [Sept. 1, 1851]: 258.
[4] Orson F. Whitney, Life of Heber C. Kimball [Salt Lake City: Kimball Family, 1888] 332–3.

Light; instantaneous and absolute knowing replaced any question I had. Still, my earthly mind was confined to a thimble in the infinite ocean of wisdom of which I became a part. In a single blink of the eternities, I learned about the true nature of God, the laws of the universe, and our relationship to it all, and so will you one day - I promise. "Death" will be the most infinitely delicious, unimaginably blissful crescendo to your life - guaranteed better than anything you have ever experienced in this realm. You will heartily laugh at yourself, at how so seriously you fussed over any single aspect of your life. Though most cannot imagine it for the rest of eternity, you will hardly ever think another thought about this lifetime, for you will always be becoming and looking forward to more. There is so much more I could explain on every topic imaginable, so much that you may not want to believe. The higher laws are for you to unlock for yourself when you are ready. I have zero desire to try and convince anyone of anything because when you know something, you do not care if everyone in the whole world does not agree with you. I have a knowing, the only kind of knowing that comes from direct experience. Only those who doubt become uncomfortable or upset when a different perspective is given. The best I can do is guide you to your guidance, for that is the pathway to all the mysteries of heaven and earth.

This book is the foundation of all that I had access to when I was with The Light. I will present the best evidence I have found on this earth to support my story.

Chapter I
—— **Myths and Misunderstanding the Nature of God** ——

I kept wondering how not a single description of God, even mine, could ever come close to the glory, power, wisdom, and unconditional love of this being. Though on earth, there seem to be as many versions of God as there are perceivers. Even from my own experience, I realized there were different versions of God that I held in some format or another. Many, including my former self, held several of these viewpoints of God on any given topic. If you hear someone's prayer, you can usually tell which version of God they are praying to at the moment.

Master & Slave

Myth: God is the master or boss, and the human is the slave or employee. Whatever scraps we can beg or earn, we are grateful. God commands: "Jump!" Our reply is, "How high?" Whatever will be; will be. The hard work for God shall be done. Whatever thy will. I have no power, no desires of my own, only to be a meek, humble, and worthy servant.

Santa Claus - Genie - Butler - Taskmaster

Myth: A prayer is more of a wish list where one can reveal to God everything that is wanted. We have a revelation for God and a list of things for Him to do. Bless the following: the sick, the missionaries, the food, those traveling, and everyone else here and not here while you are at it. Oh, and happiness and wealth? Give those to me! You know how you said this earth was "very good?" Well, you were mistaken, it is not very good anymore, it is horrible, and I have some advice for you to fix it! So, God, get a pen and paper because I've made a list, and I will think of some more tasks later today for you to do."

This is a sort of the opposite of the Boss & Employee misconception, where God becomes the worker and the person the director.

Parent & Needy Child

Myth: God is like a weary parent; if one complains long, loud, and hard enough, God will relent and give what is wanted, much like the parent giving into the screeching child in a grocery store. If someone squeaks, loud enough, long enough, and justifies a good enough case, then, and only then, will God deliver.

Vending Machine God

Myth: Insert the tokens in the form of prayer. Not receiving? Keep inserting more and more tokens of vain, repetitious, "faithful" prayers. If that is not working, try "temple tokens;" prayers offered at the temple or on the prayer rolls. Still not working? Try "fasting and prayer" or "priesthood" tokens. If that does not work, try pleading a case to others to influence them to put in some of their tokens, preferably ones with fasting, temple, and/or priesthood stamped on them. If enough tokens are put in, and I push the right buttons, then I will receive what I want.

Reality:

I had a mix of all of these notions about God. In hindsight, I can see how so many of the myths I believed showed my basic and personal lack of faith—as if I thought that the all-knowing God was not aware of all that I wanted. I showed a complete lack of faith when I repeatedly asked because apparently, He needed reminders in His old age.

In comparison, when ordering in a restaurant, I showed more faith in a waitress than I did in God Almighty. I never reminded the waiter or waitress dozens of times before the meal was served of what I ordered. When I put an order online with a reputable store, I did not keep putting in the order again and again. I certainly thought I somehow needed to remind God. Now, I see that asking again and again not only showed my complete lack of faith, but it was the reason what I wanted was not yet in my life.

I think these are probably the most popular misconceptions in the LDS world as well. I spent much of my time effectively shaking the vending machine God, "Hurry up! I've done all that has been asked of me. I've put in more than the required amount; now give me what I want!" In an instant, with The Light, I knew that these were all myths propagated by those who do not have direct experience with God or how the universe works. While it is true God loves with unconditional love and is ready to help, there are eternal laws of the universe that organize and dictate all other aspects of life, irrespective of persons. God can and will help us within the laws, but He cannot break any eternal laws, no matter how faithfully we ask. Since the purpose of this life is joy, and He wants us to be happy, we need to be in harmony to hear God's guidance within the laws.

Misunderstanding the Scriptural Personality of God

The first scriptural misconception about God, which became utterly laughable to me, was what I call "Old Testament God."

Both ancient and modern scriptures and prophets seem to have two main differing opinions about the nature of God. Most people have not read every single page of the Old Testament, but the Old Testament God is wrathful, jealous, angry, racist, one who holds grudges, prejudice, repents (for sins committed?), is a respecter of persons, and a conditional lover.

For example, using no conjecture, only hard numbers directly out of the text in the Old Testament, God killed over two million people in a vengeful rage, while Satan killed ten - not ten million - ten people.

And then, suddenly, in the New Testament, God's personality is loving, charitable, peaceful, kind, and infinitely forgiving. Which is the correct version of God? Both are 100% scriptural. How is this possible for an "unchangeable" being? An interesting research project has helped answer that question for me.

In 2010 there was a groundbreaking study that dove into people's beliefs about the viewpoint of God.[5] The study participants were asked their opinion about some controversial moral issues like war, abortion, drugs, etc. The questions asked pertained to what the "average American" thought about these issues, compared to their viewpoints, and finally, what they thought God thinks on the same topic. These were not merely surveys. During these questionnaires, the study participants were inside functional magnetic resonance imaging (fMRI) machines. The scientists looked at the actual areas of the brains and the synapses that lit up when the subjects thought about and answered the questions. Then the scientists found an interesting revelatory correlation: when any participant was asked the question, "What do you think..." versus "What does God think...?" the same areas of the brain lit up as if they were asked the same question. **Everyone viewed that God had the same opinions that they had on every topic.** This happened to everyone, regardless of race, gender, religion, or age, to 100% of the people 100% of the time. As it turns out, this is a condition of human nature; it is hardwired in the very fabric of how our brains translate information.

With everyone translating the nature of God into their own image, the question worth pondering is: Were the people of the Old Testament any different?

It is impossible to blame thousands of descriptions of interactions with Old Testament God be all "mistranslation" errors. It is apparent that either God is a schizophrenic, changeable being or, just like modern-day science has confirmed, that all people indeed create God in their own image. It is not that the true nature of God was "mean" in the Old Testament and suddenly "nice" in the New Testament; it was that the people of the Old Testament were mostly

---

[5] Waytz, A., Morewedge, C., Epley, N., Monteleone, G., Gao, J., & Cacioppo, J.T. 2010. "Making sense by making sentient: Effectance motivation increases anthropomorphism." Journal of Personality and Social Psychology, *99*, 410-435.

vengeful, racist, prejudiced, conditional lovers, and wrathful, and therefore, the God they made in their own image was too. And God allowed it because He understands life is an evolutionary process of line upon line. It was not until The Light came along, who was Jesus, that we started to receive an accurate representation of who God really is; peaceful, kind, and unconditionally loving. Justly so, Jesus was more like God than were the mere mortals of the Old Testament.

Instead of arguing over which ancient scripture is true or studying fMRI brain scans, there is a better way: have your own spiritual experience. Sometime in the future, sit down for a time with no distractions and clear your mind of all worries and thoughts. Take several deep, slow breaths; focus deep down inside. Ask the eternal part of yourself, the part of you that is connected to God, to teach you the truth of these two scripturally accurate statements once and for all:

"God is angry. God is wrathful. God is racist. God is prejudiced. God holds grudges. God is a respecter of persons. God is offendable. God is a conditional lover. God is moody and will kill millions for spite."

Or

"God is love. God is kind. God is infinitely forgiving; God is charitable. God is peaceful. God is joy. God is happy. God is bliss. God is unoffendable. God is all-powerful. God is all-knowing."

Which one of those phrases felt right to you? Which one felt good and tugged at your soul with delightful confirmation - and which one did not feel right? Which one felt off to you? Which one did not make sense at a soul level?

This has profound repercussions on all gospel teachings around the world. True, it seems difficult, even overtly blasphemous, to even hint that a prophet, modern or ancient, could be off about the nature of God. However, no mortal will ever really understand God until we reunite with Him. Our mortal limitations cannot comprehend even a fraction of the mysteries of the infinite universe.

Besides, this provides an insight into the psychological projection of people whenever a description of God's personality is offered; one can see so much more into that person than into the actual nature of God. If someone offers a description of God as offendable, non-forgiving, and at times angry, one can be assured they are offendable, non-forgiving, and sometimes angry too.

Today, most of the Old Testament God is ignored, justly so. Lesson outlines in most Christian denominations will skirt around any scriptures that convey a God who is acting ungodly. To paraphrase J.B.S. Haldane: "God is not stranger than we think he is; he is stranger than we can think." Mortal minds can never understand the nature of God.

It is true that making this kind of judgment on great prophets may be too much for many to bear. However, it is unknown how someone reconciles the vast personality differences between the God of the Old and New Testaments.

It is my absolute knowledge that there is not a shred of any hate, disgust, judgment, wrath, offendableness, vengefulness, prejudice, racism, or even the least bit of anything non-virtuous in The Light. He is all pure, all love, all bliss, non-stop, forever and ever, and has been throughout all time. All the scriptures in the world will never convince me, in a million years, otherwise.

> *He that loveth not knoweth not god; for God is love.*
> *John 4:8*

Misunderstanding the Personality of God versus The Eternal Laws of the Universe.

As I was filled with countless questions during the panorama of my life, I saw countless interactions in which I wondered why this infinitely loving Being, who has all power, did not intervene in my life. As soon as I thought about the question, the answers filled my being with a perfect understanding of The Laws.

Clearly Defining the Laws of the Universe

In the scriptures, humanity described acts of God as a blanket term that included everything they misunderstood: weather anomalies, change in seasons, animal migration, illnesses, injuries, disease, planetary motion, death, birth gender, skin color; the list is endless. Everything humankind experienced was from God (good and bad) either as a blessing or a punishment for something they, or someone nearby, did or did not do. However, they were more than a little confused. Only with the clarity of the Book of Mormon do we start to learn about the laws and how they are separate from God. Almost all of the misunderstandings about the true nature of God are encompassed in the misunderstanding between the eternal, unchanging laws of the universe and the personality of the eternal being. We are the only religion that even preaches that God is bound by laws too and that He would "cease to be God" (Alma 29:4) if He did not abide by them.

Consequences are affixed to every action– spiritual, temporal, tangible, and intangible. It is impossible for even God to break the laws of the universe. He knows the laws with perfection and works with and within the laws. I realized that the majority of prayers offered in this world, including my own up until that point, were typically people praying to have God break the laws of the universe for them. This entire universe is based on cause and effect, action and reaction. Frankly speaking, and not merely spoken enough, this law is sometimes called the Law of the Harvest. Nephi explained some of the basic tenants of the law.

"And now, my sons, I speak unto you these things for your profit and learning; for there is a God, and he hath created all things, both the heavens and the earth, and all things that in them are, both things to act and things to be acted upon." ~2 Nephi 2:14

All laws of the universe are similar to the Law of the Harvest. Fruit bears seeds that will bear more of the same fruit. These laws of the universe are unchanging; "the same yesterday, today and forever," part of what humankind clumped together as "God." These laws operate irrespective of wickedness or righteousness. After a man falls off a cliff, whether he be righteous or wicked, gravity will pull him to his death.

I had never learned what the Law of the Harvest was in any great detail. And yet, with The Light, I saw it commanding every single aspect of every single interaction of every single second of each life. Using the analogy of the harvest is simple because it is tangible. It is simple to understand that if a cherry seed is properly planted and tended to, it will yield more of the same - cherries. From cats come kittens, acorns become oak trees, and a person of light will attract more light; more of the same comes from the same. Never does one plant strawberry seeds and harvest a puppy. It is the law.

The physical aspect is painfully elementary, yet, the same laws apply to all intangible creations and interactions as well. Never does one sow seeds of fear, hate and worry and harvest bliss, love, and joy. There are millions of types of tangible plants and animals on earth; however, there are countless more intangible fruits that all humans harvest each day.

Jesus taught that fruits have a purpose, and everything is a fruit: your relationships, your bank account balance, your mood, your health, everything. God does not differentiate between spiritual and temporal, as "...all things unto me are spiritual..." (D&C 29:34). "All things" does not leave out much.

Tangibly speaking, it is simple to understand that every object surrounding everyone right now was once someone's thought. The real revelation to me was how everything, including intangible things, comes into our lives through our thoughts as well. I saw that it was never God sending or withholding to or from us or ever sending trials or challenges. Everything we receive is the fruit we planted, mostly unknowingly. Like it says many times in the Book of Mormon, punishments, and blessings are "affixed," just like the type of fruit is affixed to the type of seed. Bitter fruits are never "sent" from a moody or angry God. Those were all fruits that we thought into being, on a spiritual essence first.

In wondering how it all worked, a City of Light Being opened to my mind's eye a city which I had never been to before or seen. Real or not, I do not know. It was bustling with countless people and their interactions; each was giving me an example of how it all worked. I could see another part of our dimension where I could see a harmonic frequency, like colored energy, that surrounded people. I saw different levels of light or energy around people that originated from the thoughts they were thinking. Their words had minuscule power compared to their thoughts; it was as if I had an insight into their very hearts and intentions. Sometimes words were even the opposite of someone's thoughts. Many people affirmed they were having a good day but inwardly felt so very different. I also noticed that the people associated only with people with very similar colors of light or levels of energy. I immediately noticed that light indeed attracts light, similar shades, colors, and patterns of it. I saw similar groups going together and interacting with each other - sort of like schools of fish that only traveled with their kind. Some were dimmer than others comparatively, and yet, I knew that all energy could not assert itself into another as this was the basis of the laws. The basis for the laws was, in one word: harmony. Everything was all about harmony.

I noticed that it was not only people with light or energy harmony, but it was also with objects as well; everything had intelligence and shade of energy pattern. The Light passed no judgment, and I saw there was no hierarchy - no one better than another - from The Light's perspective. A "nice" house was filled with "nice" things and was lived in by "nice" people. All the colors matched up in harmony. I saw that some people could look at a person from a distance and would love and appreciate them, and in/with those thoughts, they became harmonious with loving people. Others would perceive the same people, and they wanted it as well, but they radiated in opposite harmony; they had mixed feelings of jealousy, resentment, and anger about it. As I watched the light energy change and saw the disharmony, everything at once became clear to me. People needed to change their thought harmony to match objects to start receiving them. It was a matter of changing the thoughts to become similar to those of people who had what they wanted. A shift in thinking to become more like something else is all it would take, and that could be done very fast, as I saw how quickly thoughts changed. It does not take long to hear a different song when you change the tuner. However, few people had consistent patterns of thought across all aspects of their life. They were a mix of different patterns of harmony with every single aspect of life. Some things they loved–they were in harmony with. Other things they wanted–they were not in harmony with. So, while everything was in flux and constantly changing, it was changing from the same to more of the same and then changing to more of the same again. People mostly associated with others with the same patterns of thought, which in turn just served to reinforce more of the same. People with vastly different energies were very disharmonious, like the difference between an employee and a successful owner of a company. Employees did not dislike the boss per se; the two groups just had incongruous energy–they were not in harmony. It expressed itself into the physical by the two liking different things, talking about different subjects, and having differing

15

interests. Birds of a feather indeed flock together on a very intangible energy basis. I could see that forcing people together rather than letting people gravitate never would turn out well. The Light was beaming with delight and loving joy to confirm my understanding.

Within my complete awareness of this city, I noticed that babies and very little children were the brightest and clearest. It is difficult to describe; they radiated most similarly to The Light. Though not verbal, they also had simple desires that they harmonized with and were fulfilled. They were very powerful in obtaining what they wanted, and they knew this was the way it was supposed to be. I could see their clarity and power. However, little children very soon adopted the energy of the people who surrounded them, usually their parents. Worried parents had the dimmest light (or furthest harmony) from The Light, and the children suffered for it in all aspects of their life–physically, socially, and emotionally. This is where I saw that it was all going wrong. I changed my awareness back towards The Light to seek answers; I was lovingly reminded that nothing was going wrong here. All interactions were products of law and not of God's fickle choosing, and all was good in His eyes.

I then wondered about all those prayers I had offered and my attempts to influence God. In typical fashion, all that I desired to know was presented to me yet again, in the most perfect way possible. I loved learning in this way; there was nothing I could not understand. I had access to everything.

I then saw countless people praying, or rather in the physical act of prayer, because, in most prayers, I saw people's harmony fluctuating everywhere. Being in prayer was not much different from normal walking around, harmonically speaking. They thought of what they wanted but then realized they did not have it yet, begged God for it, and oddly, I could see ripples of their thoughts into their future. Their disharmonious thoughts pushed whatever they wanted away from their energy. It was like they were trying to tune to a certain radio station and hear a song but moved the dial and only occasionally tuned into snippets of it. They were so conflicted in their thoughts: the desire to have whatever God wanted them to have, the desire to have faith, the desire to influence God, guilt for wanting more, and anger for not having it while others did. But mostly, it was their conscious realization that they did not have what they wanted. This disharmony kept all things from coming into their life. For years to decades to even a lifetime, I saw the ripples of their thoughts to their future. Then I saw another who gave up asking and stopped being so aware of the lack of what he wanted that it came right into his experience. I remembered this in my own life. We called it "ironic," but it was entirely law-based harmony. What was more disturbing was that this disgruntled awareness was like cancer in their life. The more they thought about all they did not have, the more it spread to all other aspects of their life, and they had less and less of what they wanted. Then I understood: our thoughts of absence keep perpetuating absence because there is a specific harmony of absence and a separate harmony of presence to all things.

Immediately after I understood how it did not work and how I had been doing it wrong my whole life, I started to become more aware of those who were living more joyful lives. I saw that they were in joy most of the time and worked to look at everything in this positive light. I also saw another group that looked like they were praying as well, but these people were bright and steady in their energy, growing more like The Light's energy. They were connecting to it and drawing from it in true harmony. It wasn't in the quantity or intensity of words or thoughts but the absence of them. In the silence of all worldly thoughts, worries, and concerns, they returned to harmony with open communication from God. This did not make any sense to me until I saw the ripples of their actions. They had The Light's energy and power with them in their interactions far greater than most others. This brilliant light attracted more light. While life inspired their desires just like it did for everyone else, and because they had spent so much time in harmony with The Light, they literally did not see or experience such undesirable events because they had no harmony with them. They were not monks; they were not chanting in robes or lying on beds of nails; they just sat each day quietly, and in the absence of all the worrisome chatter in their minds, in that peace was their connection to The Light. They had the same light little children had.

When people generally harmonized with what they judged as good, all things that were in harmony with good steadily drew closer to them. When people harmonized with what they judged as bad, all things that were bad steadily drew nearer to their experience. Whatever people thought about it, I could see the spiritual creation; it was created as soon as they experienced the opposite of it. When someone is in pain, that is when they ask for relief. When people believed it was simple to have something, like when they could go to the store and purchase it, they harmonized quickly and found a way fast. When they believed it was difficult, no harmony was experienced, and nothing came to them. I could see that if they kept their thoughts in harmony, all kinds of unseen forces helped move the object, like a magnet, closer to their future path. There are far more people and forces helping us than we realize if we have that harmony. Harmony was like they were tuned into a classical station; while all the songs were different, they were all good and in harmony. People who could keep their thoughts positive received more positive things. But most people just looked around and thought about what they saw, with no discipline to keep it positive in the face of non-harmonious things.

"Bad" things to "Good" People?

For as he thinketh in his heart, so is he.
Proverbs 23:7

I now saw the answer to the world's age-old question, "Why could God allow this to happen?" Or "Why do bad things happen to good people?" Even hundreds of years before Christ, people were asking this question of God, called "The Problem of Evil." Epicurus wrote this in 341 BC:

Is God willing to prevent evil but not able? Then he is not omnipotent.

Is he able but not willing? Then he is malevolent.

Is he both able and willing? Then whence cometh evil?

Is he neither able nor willing? Then why call him God?

All can relate to Epicurus when their life is going in an unexpected and undesired direction or when they are witnessing a seemingly awful act. This has been part of the basis of the battle-cry of the atheist for thousands of years. The logic is indeed flawless, but the premise of God by Epicurus is gravely flawed. He is mistaking the "how" (laws) for the "whom" (God). The logic also underlines the main reason so many people do not understand God, dislike all religions, and how most in the church have a Santa-Claus-Genie-Wish-Granting-Vending-Machine view of God like I did.

First, Epicurus did not realize that nothing in the entire universe ever happens outside the law of the harvest. If people sow and tend to certain seeds yet pray with their words to receive a different type of fruit other than what was planted, nothing can ever change. No matter how righteous the person or how many prayers are offered, God's hands are tied. Secondly, asking, "Is God willing or able to prevent evil?" Here "evil" is a judgment. It is impossible for mortals to judge "bad" or "good" things. Jesus taught "Judge ye not" because there is no possible way mortals can see the whole story. It does not take more than a few years of mature life experience to be entirely convinced that a past "horrible" event that was judged as "evil" (that you cried to God to remove) was, in fact, one of the best things that could have happened to you. The God that Epicurus speaks of is entirely fictional.

With the infinite wisdom and eternal perspective of God, "Is God willing and or able to prevent evil?" God allows all to happen to everyone per the laws of the universe; free agency was the reason the war in heaven was fought. There is no other way. God's role is not to change the laws of the universe or to enforce them. Many religions think that God is all-knowing and just watching everything unfold. Many religions were built around that fact and came up with theories like the doctrine of predestination. This came about by attempting to pray and noticing God was always out to lunch–because nothing ever happened with any consistency. They did not realize they were probably asking God to change the laws. Thus, they never asked for anything; everything bad or unwanted that came into their life was God's will. The other side is petitioning a magical wizard in the sky to wave his magic wand to change every single aspect of life, requesting that some of the consequences of their choices will not come to fruition. Both aspects are alive and well in most people today, albeit quite mixed together.

The true relationship with God

After defining more distinctly the laws of the universe and what is not the nature of God, what is our true relationship with God?

God's part as the "enforcer of the law of the universe" is as ridiculous as gravity police making sure things do not fall up. God does not spend his time making sure the correct fruits come from the same seeds. God is indeed a dynamic being; otherwise, we would not have had the lower set of the Law of Moses change to a higher, more love-based law. If He did not answer your prayer yesterday, then He would not today or ever. God has promised us that he will assist us in "whatsoever ye desire," yet, the laws are irrespective of God; therefore, God's part lies in **guidance**.

"We are co-creators with God."[6] When I read this from J. Richard Clarke, I immediately knew this General Authority knew God. We are partners. The laws are an unchangeable environment. God is directing each of our guidance, which does respond to our intentions. All must be in tune with the laws. We are the captain of the destination. God is the navigation. The environment is where we both come together for joyful co-creation.

What is our part?

We are allowed agency or freedom to decide where we think we want to go, even if our destination will not be all that we thought it would be. We then learn that lesson and continue from where we are in the moment. God knows the best route working within the laws to guide us to where we think we want to end up. Besides, eternal beings will never be finished, so any place we are is just another step along the way.

"I ought not to harrow up in my desires, the firm decree of a just God, for I know that he granteth unto men according to their desire, whether it be unto death or unto life; yea, I know that he allotted unto men, yea, decreeth unto them decrees which are unalterable, according to their wills, whether they be unto salvation or unto destruction." ~Alma 29:4

While nobody truly desires death and destruction, the point of

---

[6] The Value of Work - Ensign 1982 May

the scripture is that no matter what one focuses on, it shall be granted. It is law, and there are no exceptions to these laws. Would an infinitely loving and omniscient God grant people who are praying for death and destruction their desires? Has anyone ever prayed for death and destruction to come upon them? This is talking about Universal laws, not God's personality, which are two items often confused or combined. The "unalterable" part is they receive "according to their will." But who "wills" unwanted things? It is not that they "will it" consciously; it is what they focus their attention on. It is the law of the harvest. If you focus and harmonize with Godly things, you will yield fruits of God such as love, charity, kindness, knowledge, confidence, power, bliss, and, more importantly, all things that will make you feel that way. If you focus on ungodly things such as fear, hate, revenge, worry, or sadness, you will yield ungodly fruits. It is the law.

We can choose anything we want–wickedness or happiness. We guide our boat and plant our seeds, but we are limited in the "arm of flesh" if we want wicked things for ourselves or others. If we want to create wonderful things, we have access to the power that created the entire universe when we are in harmony with it. To access that power, we need to harmonize with God. To fulfill our purpose in life, we need to be in tune with God so we can hear the guidance.

Chapter II
How God Communicates With Us

In the City of Light, I saw how everything was so harmonious. Rivers of harmonious energy patterns flowed to and from everything. Redirecting my focus on one joyful person, I could see how they were going to rendezvous with all kinds of fantastic, delightful, and good things–joyful and fun interactions, satisfying business deals, etc. And others, I just knew by looking at their harmonic energy that horrible things were coming–illnesses, car wrecks, rude people, and all things that were in harmony within the spectrum of energy they held. They were harmonious fruits that grew logically from the thought seeds they were tending. With each minute of focus, they inched closer and closer to tangible fruit.

So similar to a radio station that only plays one genre; while all the songs are different, they are also all similar. If a young woman was angry at men, she'd kept rendezvousing with men who would make her angrier at men. This genre of anger followed her in almost every interaction all day, every day, and anger was where she set her dial.

A wealthy man basked in appreciation at good things coming in; thus, he could keep pulling in large amounts of money. This love and appreciation followed him around as more things to love and appreciate were his song. Everything spiraled downward or upwards based on their mere attention.

What shocked me was how two people walking down the same street would only see things that they were in harmony with. In other words, those people who were mostly "negative" would miss all the beauty that surrounded them. The opposite was true as well, but these infinite variations of energy responded to every aspect of their life, from how they slept to which waitresses they had, each pocket of traffic which they traveled, what customers they met, and when they met up with their friends and family. If someone was angry only a fraction of the time and someone else always expected angry people in their life, they would both meet up when anger was in both of them.

As I saw all the interactions, everything made perfect sense. I kept realizing, "Of course that happened to him–of course, that happened to her." And God allowed all of it, with nothing but loving understanding, basking in the knowledge that it was all good. God knew that each experience helped to clarify more desires, and without the questions being asked, no answers could be given.

This was the evolution of life, and without it all, we would be damned, and all progression would stop. I knew that somehow, we, in our oneness, were part of the evolution of God.

I then felt a splendid, loving, disharmonious direction from The Light that I was the one incorrectly judging these events as horrible or delightful. They were just indicators of where their thoughts had taken them. Never did God send "lessons" or "trials" to anyone. That would not only make God a conditional lover, a changeable being, and a respecter of persons but a violator of Universal Law. Not even God can make a kitten grow where a pumpkin seed was planted. Certainly, one can attempt to find lessons in every event; I saw that the only real lesson to be learned is this: **what comes into your life because of the thoughts you were thinking.**

When I saw people holding an awful thought, an awful feeling came to indicate how their thoughts were not in alignment with God. At that moment, The Light brought to my understanding this was His way of communicating with us. The bad or painful feelings were of disharmony to indicate we *needed to change our thoughts. Our feelings are like a relationship to God's viewpoint barometer. How The Light communicates with everyone in every moment is through our emotions. Good means God is in agreement, and bad means God does not agree. It was so simple, yet I never understood this built-in system of inner connection to God at all times.*

Purpose of emotions

Evolutionarily speaking, it is simple to understand the purpose of the five senses; sight, smell, hearing, touch, and taste. I now saw what the God-given purposes of emotions were and how similar they are to our other senses.

Imagine a primitive version of yourself, running around a forest or jungle. If you intended to cross a raging river, life intact, your eyes would help you see the best path to take and any dangers ahead of you. Your God-given sense of sight allows you to know before each step so that adjustments can be made accordingly.

If you intended to eat something nutritious and beneficial and came across something that looked delicious, but when you picked it up smelled rancid, that is your God-given sense of smell revealing to you that the path you are on (what you are about to eat) will not yield the desired results.

In the same manner, if you intended to get something to eat and came across something that looked plump and delicious and did not smell bad, but when you put it in your mouth, it tasted like fire, that is your God-given sense of taste telling you that the path you are on will not yield you the results that you want.

If you intended to get something to drink, hearing the trickling stream would tell you water is near. Or, if you intend continued existence, hearing a dangerous animal coming your way is your God-given sense of hearing telling you that the dangerous animal-filled path you are on will not yield you the results that you want.

The emotions or feelings sometimes called the sixth sense, are a bit more complex to deconstruct. Few, if any, are born entirely emotionally blind–all feel good and bad. In an identical manner to all your other five senses, your emotions indicate whether or not you are in alignment with your desires and in harmony with God's guidance.

With all before me and with my new awareness of the laws and our emotions, I remembered when I loved unconditionally (which entirely consisted of the early stages of a relationship when I was a teenager). During these times, I was in complete harmony with God's light. It was unmistakable. The feelings of unconditional love, the viewpoint that I held in which this person could do no wrong, I was joining in God's same viewpoint. In those thoughts, I was one with God. The factor that was so interesting was that it felt amazing–not because the person was really wonderful, but because of my harmony with God's viewpoint. When one sees through the eyes of God, there is no better feeling. **We call this Love.**

On the other end of the scale, when I looked at someone with hate and anger, I was in complete disharmony with God. I thought I had negative feelings of hate for them because they were "not a nice person," but it was because I was entertaining a thought with which God did not agree. So, I had an empty feeling and blamed the person for it. It was the painful void of disharmony with God.

All people are using external things or thoughts as a sort of reason to be in or out of harmony with God. Emotions always come as an indicator of thoughts, and thoughts come first, not emotions. When we think we are unworthy, bad, and no good, the empty feeling comes from God not joining us in our thoughts.

> *"When we direct our thoughts properly, we can control our emotions*
> *~W. Clement Stone"*

An indicator reading is neither good nor bad. All of your vehicle's indicator gauges: check engine, near-empty fuel tank, oil light, are not evil when lit up and righteous when off–they just 'are.' If nearing empty fuel, if the light is ignored, the journey may not continue on the intended path uninhibited. Emotions work in the same way. If we desire a relationship and think about how fun it would be and all of the pleasant mutual experiences we will have, we feel great, and our emotions soar. This is God telling us we are on the right path, thinking the right thoughts, and if we keep thinking these thoughts, our desires will come to fruition. Conversely, when we think about how we are alone, how all the good ones are taken, and what or who we do not have yet, we feel bad because God does not agree with us in those thoughts.

When someone says "control your emotions," that is like saying "control your low fuel gauge indicator," which is bad advice because nobody really can or would want to control or ignore it. Someone cannot hate someone else and receive the indicator of harmony with God. Asking someone to control their emotions is like asking your car to restrain itself and not light up the low fuel indicator when approaching empty. One must change the thoughts; then, the emotional indicators will change.

How to change thoughts

I saw people in the middle of strong thoughts but only having access to similar thoughts, a little better or a little

27

worse–like they stood in the middle of a huge rainbow–and could only go to colors a little bit darker and a little bit brighter from where they were. Or, in the middle of a staircase, they had the freedom to move, but they could only go up or down a step. It was exactly like an old-fashioned analog radio dial (before presets), where if one wanted to change what was being heard, one must start from wherever they were and move upwards or downwards incrementally. To move to the top, one must pass through everything in the middle.

I saw a woman that was very similar to The Light observing some children playing with toys. One child took another's toy, and he was furious and hit the toy thief. The woman came over and sat with the toy-less child. The child must not have been her own because the boy expected retribution for hitting. She spoke with him and empathized with the child, agreeing that when someone took away his toy, he felt sad, became angry, and sought revenge by hitting. I could not believe that she basically condoned the hitting. However, this soothed the child, and his energy brightened a little bit. The woman talked and continued, eventually moving the child from less and less anger to just being bothered and annoyed. The conversation went something similar to this: "Eventually, he will put down the toy, and you can play with it. You know he's not going to play with it forever," and there was a flash of hope now in the boy. She continued, "...and there are lots of other fun toys to play with like...." and with that, the boy had joyfully engaged again, and he knew it would be all right. I did not understand why this interaction was before us until I remembered how subtly she changed the aura of the child from dim to bright.

She was a genius, and she understood the laws. Most parents would have scolded the offending child and commanded him not to hit. A seemingly more loving approach would be to tenderly say that the children should love each other and be nice to each other or how his actions made the other child feel. But love is so far away from anger–almost opposite–that it is too far of a leap to initially traverse; this would send children into darker places, feeling powerless, because they did not have the choice of love available from where they were in anger.

> *...doubt not, but be believing...*
>
> *Mormon 9:27*

I now see how the best way to help a friend who is inconsolably sad is to help them to anger, at least temporarily. Think of yourself; would not you rather enjoy plotting vengeance compared to being inconsolably destitute? Is there anything more annoying in the entire world than when you are angry, and someone tells you, "You should just be happy?" The steps are too far apart, like at the end of a long staircase. To climb to the top, you have to move up one step at a time. The goal is not to stay in revenge and act; it just allows someone a little more of one's light and power back so that they can breathe easier again. They are one step closer to who they really are. Eventually, the life-giving conversation about vengeful thoughts will lose steam and momentum. You will notice a lull in the conversation as all that anger is now out and done. A person can then move to be just embittered, followed by dissatisfied, and then irritated, then maybe slight optimism, ending in knowing that everything will be alright because whatever does not kill you makes you stronger and smarter than before. Each step gave a little relief. And in as simple as a single conversation, you can help a friend move to better thoughts and, thereby, a better feeling place. It can take a few minutes or even an hour. Larger problems may take a month, but this is what therapists often cannot do in decades because condemning a step in the right direction (anger from depression) is labeled as "inappropriate." And talking about the problem amplifies and prolongs it because they maintain harmony with it through their focus. However, society may label it: a step in the right direction is a step in the right direction. Helping someone to anger from depression is being a true friend, as long as you do not stop at anger.

Some people never leave the anger behind because they are trying to either jump too far ahead (to a better feeling place) or they are condemned for their anger which makes them spiral downward from anger to depression (back to being without hope). The road goes both ways; if someone is mildly annoyed, guiding them into vengeful thoughts is the wrong way. The gospel is not a gospel of instantaneous destination but a journey where one becomes incrementally a little better.

What is sin and the true purpose of commandments

While looking at all these people who held negative thoughts about themselves and others and moved (or tuned out) from their natural, harmoniously-aligned-with-God, loving selves, I was shocked to hear The Light volunteer: This is real sin.

It wasn't until I studied the term "sin" and discovered that in Aramaic, it means 'to separate.' And that is exactly what we do when we hold unloving, angry, worried, or hateful thoughts–we separate ourselves from God. When John Calvin translated the Bible himself, without the permission of the Roman Catholic Church, he found that historically, "sin" was later used as an archery term, meaning "missed the mark," not something that offended God requiring restitution. The mark is the goal of being in harmony with God so that we can do and be all which is possible: "For with God, all things are possible." I always thought sin meant something that offended God, but this Being of Light...offendable? It could never be. If it is virtuous to be unoffendable, I know God has it. This Being of Light lacked not a single virtue.

I now wondered how or if The Light forgave these sins, as he never seemed upset about them. They did not seem like typical "sins" because everyone was thinking most of the time thoughts that separated themselves from God or what they wanted. And with the same sort of heavenly laughter, He opened my eyes to the awareness that He did not need to forgive them because He had never condemned them in the first place.

Today, this has become my goal in life: never forgive anyone because I never condemn them in the first place. Is it better to become proficient at removing bullets from your body (forgive quickly), or just not shoot yourself in the first place (not condemning), thereby not needing to remove the bullet? One may choose, "I forgive quickly." I will choose "never condemn." This is a higher law. It cannot always be a conscious choice, as will be discussed in Chapter 6, but it is possible.

There is an infinitude of higher laws as it makes sense for eternally evolving beings. 'Eye for an eye becomes 'love your enemy.' Higher than 'love your enemy' is 'have no enemies.' Higher than 'have no enemies' is 'what is an enemy?" Imagine one day trying to explain what the word 'enemy' means to a child, and they just do not understand why they would not like someone for any reason. What a glorious day that would be!

Sinning, (as separating oneself from God) makes the saying entirely true: "You are not punished for your sins; you are punished by your sins." You are not punished for your anger (by a vengeful condemning offendable God); you are punished by your anger (by the lack of spiritual communion with God in moments of anger). Just as a child learning to walk stumbles (misses the mark of stable walking or technically sins), no parent condemns the child and tells the child they need to repent and beg for forgiveness. In like manner, we are all learning to walk on this earth, and God, in His infinite wisdom and patience, joyfully knows that with each stumble, we are learning to find our balance. Soon we will be able to walk, then run, and then soar with God.

Is God sad or angry when we sin?

I now reflect on notions such as "nothing doth offend God more..." This notion that God is offendable, sad, disappointed, angry, or hurt when we sin, I was raised upon–and believed wholeheartedly. Now, whenever I think of The Light being offended, angry, sad, or upset– this unbelievably loving being–the notion is beyond ludicrous.

A more accurate definition of "sin" has been provided. How it became twisted through the millennium, I do not know. If you cannot take my testimony, I ask that you ponder upon a few thoughts: Using the old definition of sin, just think how many people out of the billions that are on the earth today, including the worlds without number, are sinning right now? It is pretty safe to say that someone, somewhere, is sinning every single moment of every millisecond. Now, if God is sad, disappointed, or angry when someone sins, when would God ever be happy? Also, if our goal is to become like God, do we desire this so that we can be similarly miserable for the rest of eternity? Or is it possible the schizophrenic, Old-Testament God is back, and part of Him is sad, but his other personality is mostly happy? Or maybe He is sad from 9 AM to 5 PM and has the nights and weekends off? Does that feel true?

Also, we have all lived enough life to know that some of the "worst" things that happen to us turn into the best things ever, given a little more perspective on our part. Why would an all-knowing God who has an eternal perspective be sad about the best thing happening to you ever? Besides something feeling terribly off about the idea, the truth comes into view: God is not angry or sad when we sin.

I can say with certainty The Light is observing all of us as part of us with ineffable, non-stop love. Even though our sins are keeping us from all of the benefits of being connected with The Light, He is always there patiently waiting and guiding us back to Him, nonstop, through our emotions. With the same jubilance that a parent has when watching their child take their first steps, applauding every awkward effort or flat-out failed attempt along the way, God applauds us as well and never is overcome with rage when we make mistakes or desire to punish us for making Him angry.

While God is our father, He does not act like a mortal, disharmonious-with-God, human parent. One of the biggest misconceptions about God is that He acts like a worried parent. Worry is fear; fear that someone or something is going to take away your good feeling, and God is not a fearful being, quite the opposite. God knows we will eventually find our balance and figure it all out. How long does the average earthly parent give their child to learn to walk before they give up in anger at the repeated stumbles? Succeeding is our destiny.

What is the purpose of commandments?

"For behold, it is not meet that I should command in all things; for he that is compelled in all things, the same is a slothful and not a wise servant; wherefore he receiveth no reward."
~Doctrine and Covenants 58:26

As God has a vested interest in our happiness, as we are all one, the commandments are parameters for those who do not yet have an active, in-the-moment connection to God's guiding direction. They are like training wheels to make sure we do not fall all the way down while learning to ride. In disharmonious separation from God (sin), we are left alone with the "arm of flesh," and things never turn out as well as with God. If we always had the spirit all of the time, we would not need a list of commandments. The ancient Jews had 613 commandments to guide them in every single aspect of their day, but those commandments have been fulfilled.

"In that he saith, A new covenant, he hath made the first old. Now that which decayeth and waxeth old is ready to vanish away. "
~Hebrews 8:13

The real, new commandment is to be love (see appendix). When you feel genuine love, that is an emotional indicator that your thoughts (and therefore you) are in harmony with God. When you are in tune with God, He will guide you in every situation.

"But if ye be led of the spirit, ye are not under the law.

Galatians 5:18 "

The spirit always trumps all commandments. We even have Nephi being inspired to kill Laban. If murder is permitted when inspired, then all other commandments are secondary to the spirit as well. This is deep doctrine, and I do not know how lenient any non-inspired bishop would be if someone said they felt inspired to do something not in line with the current schools of thought. I am certain it happens often; yet, if some say that God is no longer a God of inspiration, it sounds a lot like Mormon's prophecy about the unbelievers saying God is no longer a God of miracles:

"And if there were miracles wrought then, why has God ceased to be a God of miracles and yet be an unchangeable Being? And behold, I say unto you he changeth not; if so, he would cease to be God; and he ceaseth not to be God, and is a God of miracles. And the reason why he ceaseth to do miracles among the children of men is because that they dwindle in unbelief, and depart from the right way, and know not the God in whom they should trust." ~Mormon 9:19-20

Life is just too complex to try and pre-map everything to everyone in every possible situation and make a commandment about it beforehand, like from what to eat for breakfast to with whom to converse today. It is unwise to think that merely following these few general guidelines is the key to everything turning out fantastic in life. With that misunderstanding, the commandments can overpromise and underdeliver.

The majority of lifelong LDS members have been in situations in which they "followed the commandments" and did nothing "wrong" yet ended up in a horrible, unwanted situation. What makes it more frustrating is the scriptures have proclaimed, keep the commandments, and you will be blessed and will prosper in the land; disobey the commandments, and you shall be cursed.

And yet all members, in times of reflection, take a step back and realize there must be more to the story because they have not committed any huge sins and have noticed they're not more prosperous than before. While elsewhere, many are not keeping any of the "rules," and they are thriving, healthy, and wealthy. How can this be?

With no understanding or explanation of the laws of the universe, many Christian churches purport the biggest lie of all: "You must wait until after death in order to see the true rewards and punishments." Does that feel right to you? Life is not supposed to be a blind mystery. All have the light of Christ inside them to help guide with one's feelings from day one. However, the uninspired would say, "You cannot trust your feelings, listen to me instead, and I shall not lead you astray." So, the blind are then leading the blind by making them blind to their connection to God and teaching them to listen to external voices instead of their own. Those that will preach blind obedience are blind because they have no personal experience with The Light to see. If the correct laws are taught, all mysteries flutter away, and one begins to live life as they intended–connected to God. If the commandment to be love is followed, they will be inspired in all things and will prosper indefinitely.

One does not need to teach blind obedience; rather, one should teach how to connect to the Spirit, which will make all things known. Being in harmony with God is more than just keeping the rules. You can't break any commandment at the moment and still have no connection to the spirit. If everyone understood the laws of the universe, it would not be required to spread disinformation. Or, one could rationalize why things did not turn out how the scriptures promised or fabricate why God must not have seen it fit. Rather than saying prosperity, or anything, comes from directly keeping the commandments, a better answer would be, "All are receiving in accordance to their thoughts; if you are not receiving what you want, let me teach you about how to guide your thoughts to what you really want, which is an active connection to God." That is true, inspired leadership. True leaders direct to one's inner direction. False prophets say, "Follow me, and whatever you do, do not listen to that inner voice that is telling you something feels off." Missionaries' battle cry has always been "follow your feelings." Other churches will say, "Do not follow your feelings; you cannot trust them." They will throw a few devil and hell references in and add, "You must follow the Bible," meaning their interpretation of the Bible.

While it is never fair to generalize, the majority of lifelong religionists, particularly men, have been trained away from listening to their inner spirit. "Control your emotions!" is the message most men receive as little boys, which usually means, "stop listening or being affected by those emotions." Fathers sometimes do not understand their own emotions as well. While mothers teach their daughters to listen and follow their feelings, fathers will often give the battle cry of "strict obedience." Most "faithful" men will not understand someone feeling inspired to do anything, even stepping outside of the "rules." For them, it makes explanations of the story of Nephi's inspired slaying of Laban very difficult. It does not take many years to realize the one who follows inspired paths is more successful than one who follows the logic of the arm of flesh.

> *For all the law is fulfilled in one word, even in this; Thou shalt love thy neighbour as thyself.*
> *Galatians 5:14*

There are a myriad of stories about people who felt inspired not to operate within the guidelines (or commandments) at one time or another. For example, not feeling inspired to obtain a year's worth of food storage only to have the basement flood or fire destroy where the food was going to be stored. Not feeling inspired to deliver church offerings for a time, only to find out someone was embezzling the funds. Certainly, one can argue that God would still have "blessed" them for their "obedience," but what if following the spirit in all things was their goal instead of just blind obedience?

What if one's goal or intention was to have their money promptly help the poor or have their food used for themselves? Someone embezzling church funds was not in alignment with their goal, and therefore, they were God-inspired to hold off for an unknown reason which may be shown unto them later. Feeling inspired to go or do something else, instead of going to church or a class one day, only to realize months later that someone was there who said something that would have harshly offended them at that time in their life. If they came to church in the state they were in back then, it would have been detrimental to the soul. It is a hard concept to fully understand as only God perfectly understands every single intention and interaction. We can attempt to understand or have faith in God and learn to follow the spirit in all things, all places, and all times.

The bottom line is the spirit trumps all. The commandments really only apply to such a small fraction of life. We're just not confronted with the decision to kill or not kill in our daily lives. Our life is more about how and where to spend our time, with whom to interact, what thoughts to think, how to feel, what books to read, and what to say to others in certain situations.

Therefore, if you have an hour, teach guidance instead of obedience. Inner direction unlocks everything. Technically, memorizing all written commandments with perfection will help very little in any real-life situation. However, mastering guidance will direct one to do exactly what is the best and right thing to do and say in every single situation. For example, how many countless faithful LDS members followed dating standards of waiting to date until they were 16 years old, who went on LDS group dates, found a returned missionary who they married in the "right" place, at the "right" time, and who was the "right" person, only to find out that this partner was a horrible person? Conversely, had the faithful person been in tune with one's guidance, and set their intention for a joyful, co-creative, lifelong, fulfilling relationship (instead of the basic minimum requirements), and found the feeling place of that, they would have been in harmony with and found just that. The same goes for preaching more about "why you should study the scriptures" than "learning to listen to the spirit." The scriptures are records about other people and their guidance. Teaching someone how to become in alignment with God, receive their own revelation, and write their own scriptures for them is infinitely more advantageous than someone who has memorized every single scripture in existence. Study the life of Joseph Smith Jr.; all in all, he rarely taught from the Book of Mormon because when in tune, he had instantaneous guidance. An active, personal connection to God will always trump historical records about other people thousands of years ago. The answer to all questions pertaining to any life choice, like if and when to enter or leave a relationship, what field of expertise to move into, to have children or not, and how many, should all be guided by one's own inner direction. Anyone giving counsel based on other factors like gender or age should be promptly ignored as they have no experience in matters of spiritual guidance in their own life. Those without this personal relationship with the spirit will always tout scriptures, rules, norms, and mores or 'just the way we do things compared to listening to your inner guide who knows everything you want and the best path to it all.

Filling the Voids of Sin

> *I sometimes wonder whether all pleasures are not substitutes for joy*
> ~C.S. Lewis

When we are sinning, that is separating ourselves from God. We feel bad, or more accurately, the absence of good or God. On a soul level, we know we should feel joyful–it is our birthright and the purpose of life. I think we are all addicted to feeling good or feeling God so that we will always seek Him. The lack of communion with God creates a void in our soul that only companionship with God can fill. We try to fill the void with bodily addictions and a wide variety of distractions. The pleasurable feeling is counterfeit and never lasts. None of the following activities are outright "evil," as most of them have the potential for great good. However, the fruits are vastly different if these seeds are planted from a place of sin (separation from God) versus seeds planted with God. The following are some of the most common void-filling activities:

Addictive distractions include prescription drugs, alcohol, pornography, sex, food, movies/television, watching sports, computer/console gaming, internet surfing, music, romance novels, and gambling, just to name a few.

It is interesting that people who drink alcohol say there are different types of drunks: happy and angry drunks. One is drinking to enhance their experience; the other is filling voids–but both are not changing their harmony with God.

The same thing goes with all of these addictions and

distractions. Watching a ballgame can be a joyful experience, or are you watching the game because you do not like the silence?

In the quieter moments of your life, does being alone in silence with your thoughts make you uncomfortable? Do you find yourself reaching for a distraction or substance when you have nothing to do? Are we seeking a way to turn off the uncomfortable silence in the mind or change the way our body feels? I certainly did. We all do at times.

We must understand that this feeling is because we are truly addicted to the fruits of the spirit of God, and everything else falls short. It is an indicator that we need to come back to God. This is the real reason behind guiding principles like the Word of Wisdom.

Some say "moderation in all things," but this is not gospel doctrine, nor is it located in any scripture. Moderate usage of cocaine? "Inspired use of all things" is, and always will be, accurate. When fully connected and inspired by God, one would never take any substance or distract oneself to fill a void or participate in any activity that would harm another. Neither would anyone ever find themselves in a place where an opportunity would present itself because they would have been inspired to go elsewhere.

Making or spending money

Many can become obsessed with making money, which can be attributed to getting approval and/or making it easier to purchase more distractions or feed more addictions. Most incorrectly quoted, "Money is the root of all evil" when it is actually "the love of money," which is the problem. Money is not inherently evil or righteous, but you can desire money to enhance life experience or to fill a void (possibly the true root of all kinds of evil is void-filling). If you have a void that only the spirit can fill, you are going to need all the money in the world to distract you in every quiet moment of every day for the rest of your life.

Church members may also believe that if they are not breaking any commandments and going to the temple often, they are somehow in harmony with being financially 'prospered in the land.' Being in harmony with wealth has zero to do with following commandments. Therefore, if a too-good-to-be-true "business opportunity" comes along, especially from another "faithful" member, they jump at the chance. Using the logic of "he is a temple worker or a member of the 70 or a bishop" should never replace being inspired in all things.

One method of guidance is commandment-based and requires no spirit, no effort. The other method is spiritual, and one's obedience to the outward facade has no basis. If you seek business opportunities amongst friends and neighbors but cannot learn to listen to the spirit, prepare for bankruptcy or a lifetime of financial difficulty.

Shopping or purchasing another item

Buying another pair of shoes, more clothing, bags, or the latest gadget or tool may distract in the hunt, but once it is brought home, satisfaction will begin to wane, and more items will be sought after to fill the void. Countless studies have confirmed the same. If this is your personal void-filling activity, prepare for clutter in your life.

Gossiping

Trying to find the most outlandish gossip about a celebrity, friend or neighbor will keep the mind off the emptiness inside. Texting can help keep the mind off the void. The internet will help you forever be distracted from the emptiness inside. A smartphone is often very helpful with this void.

Attention from others

Another popular form of void filling is endlessly talking about a specific hardship in life, self-inflicted sufferings, or trials. Many brag about these like a badge of honor that God would find them worthy to test. Not only will this keep all the hardships in their life flowing, but the amount of time these thoughts stay on the stage of the mind will inject suffering into all other aspects of life.

Part of this activity stems from one of the popular versions of the moody-respecter-of-persons-trial sending-God. Society, oddly enough, does indeed applaud when someone digs themselves out of a hole (that they dug themselves into). People show off with pride their AA (Alcoholics Anonymous) sobriety coins that celebrate various milestones of abstinence from alcohol or drugs. However, no applause is given to one who never dug themselves in a hole, to begin with–this is the person we need to emulate and applaud.

Approval of others

Without constant contact from God, always whispering to you of your eternal and spiritual nature, you may easily associate your physical body with who you are. When someone compliments your physical appearance, it will seemingly fill the void, and you find yourself buying countless products to ensure you often receive this kind of positive attention. Spending an endless amount of time online, posting pictures of you and your family, and trying to convince yourself and others that your life is somewhat interesting or important will also distract from the spiritual void inside.

Church Service

Spending endless amounts of time in church service can be a major void-filling activity. A feeling of not being appreciated or successful at home may spur the rewarding distraction of church service. There are lots of rewarding compliments, and there is much work to accomplish. Just like everything else, if service is inspired to co-create with others in joyful ways, it is with God. If it is busy work to distract from the empty feeling inside, it is filling a void.

Having children

Many men and women want to have a joyful, child-rearing experience. Couples choose to have children to enhance their experience within a co-creative adventure or to fill voids because they feel unsuccessful in their lives. Having children to distract oneself from the unnerving feelings gnawing at you will certainly work, maybe even for a few decades to a whole lifetime, but in the quiet moments of the day, that feeling will persist and haunt you until the real problem is addressed. If not dealt with, one often transforms themselves into a busybody to further distract oneself and keep those negative feelings off the stage of the mind. Many will find that having children did not fill the void, and soon it will become a hellish experience for everyone involved. Someone having children to fill a void compared to someone having a joyful adventure will have opposite experiences. It is often those with voids that decide to have children by looking at those that are having a happy, child-rearing experience.

Getting married & dating

When two people who are living separate from an active connection and personal relationship with God come together to fill voids in each other, initially, there is great harmony and bliss because of the similarities. However, sooner rather than later, another hellish experience will ensue. Feeling empty and lonely is not a beautiful experience in and of itself, but when two empty people come together with the intent of filling voids, something exponentially uglier is created. If this is your void, save the wedding dress or tuxedo purchases for another time.

> *All sins are attempts to fill voids.*
> ~Simone Weil

When we ask the world to follow Jesus's teaching to "judge us by our fruits," it is disturbing that Utah, with a predominantly LDS population, has some rather disturbing fruits in all the major aspects of life, which all correlate directly to void-filling behavior. At the time of this writing, Utah leads the country in pornography consumption[7]

---

[7] Edelman, Benjamin. 2009. "Markets: Red Light States: Who Buys Online Adult Entertainment? *"Journal of*

(distraction, addiction) and is the fraud capital of the USA[8] (misunderstanding of harmony, inability to listen to the spirit, and/or seeking more money to more easily buy distractions or feed addictions). Mormons are heavier than non-Mormons and 34% more likely to be obese[9]. Utah has one of the highest per-capita of plastic surgeons (more than Los Angeles or New York), *the* highest consumption of cosmetics almost twelve times higher than average[10] (seeking approval), the highest consumption of psychotropic prescription drugs, and the highest rates of all forms of mental illness[11]. The divorce rate in the state has swapped from one of the lowest in the country to one of the highest in less than a generation[12].

These fruits are undeniable, and they are all direct results of a people not living with the spirit of an active connection to God. We incorrectly think that we are "God's chosen people," and He will violate the laws of the universe and give us more of the spirit than others without us having to do our part in harmonizing with God. That would make God a respecter of persons and a conditional lover. If we were connected to God, we would have a conduit of unconditional love flowing into us and our lives. We would be so full of love and light; there would be no desire to fill any void with addiction or distraction. However, the fruits are before us for the entire world to see. We must follow Christ's direction and either decide if the seed is bad (and the

Economic Perspectives, 23(1): 209-20.

[8] A 2012 article in The Economist reports that Utah is believed to have the highest per-capita rate of affinity fraud in the U.S. due to about two-thirds of the state's residents being members of the LDS Church. Authorities estimate affinity fraud cost Utahns an estimated $1.4 billion in 2010 alone, an average of about $500 per resident.
[9] Utah Health Status Survey compiled by BYU health science professor Ray Merrill, data from figures obtained in 1996, 2001 and 2003-2004.
[10] Information Resources - Spending at $9.25M vs $775K for a similarly populated area with average spending habits.
[11] Substance Abuse and Mental Health Services Administration, Center for Behavioral Health Statistics and Quality. (February 28, 2014). *The NSDUH Report: State Estimates of Adult Mental Illness from the 2011 and 2012 National Surveys on Drug Use and Health*. Rockville, MD.
[12] U.S. Census Bureau, 2010, results printed 2012 - I will personally argue that it is better to try and fail, than to never try at all. Which is what the rest of most Americans are doing by cohabitating first or never getting married. Utah has the highest marriage rates.

seed is not bad) or if it's not being planted correctly. We are taught away from following our inner guide to following things outside ourselves. We have access to tens of thousands of articles and books we can consult from thousands of religious leaders on every topic and every problem. We seek answers from the outside because we never really have heard the spirit's voice inside. We think we already have the "right" answers, so we never need to seek the spirit because everything has already been given to us.

Countless Mormons predominantly feel guilty and unworthy because they have been taught that they would prosper in the land if they kept the commandments. If they are not prospering yet keeping the commandments, they incorrectly conclude that they must not be worthy. That thought is a horrible, guilty feeling which creates voids in us that we seek to fill or hide. It feels bad precisely because God does not join us in that thought. Guilt is not of God. We are looking at ourselves in an unfavorable light, and God does not agree with that viewpoint, thus indicated by a "bad" (lack of good) feeling. Anyone using guilt as a way to motivate others toward action is never directed by God. Motivation was the devil's plan, a method of putting outside force on an object to persuade it to move. It is how the unenlightened religions of the past worked because they did not have the delicious fruits of the spirit to inspire them to be good; instead, they used threats of hell and damnation. God does not work like that. He works from the inside out via inspiration, or in-spirit–to inspire someone to act from within. When the correct knowledge of who God is and our relationship to Him is taught, we will have the fruits of the spirit fill us so completely that we will have no desire to fill voids either by artificial or insatiable means.

Doing things to fill voids will be a fleeting, pleasurable moment but will ultimately lead to a painful experience. This is due to the fruits being on opposite ends of the spectrum. Meaning, that if someone attempts to fill a void with anything besides God, it naturally leads them to spiral downward. The problem with distractions and addictions is that new, good seeds are not being nurtured; no steps toward harmony with God are made. When your thoughts are parallel

45

with God, the fruits of the Spirit are bliss, and this is the time to tend to the seedlings. Being in harmony with God is not acquired by merely not breaking the commandments (which is just a list of some of the most blatant, misaligning, separating acts of commission); one must first fill your life with God, evade the voids, and then, and only then, can inspired action take place.

Chapter III

Understanding the Purpose of Prayer

All the preceding information was laying a foundation, explaining the laws of the universe and the purpose of emotions, and how they directly relate to God and your life. It is now time to understand prayer and our part.

Broadly and basically speaking, prayer is focused thought on a subject, typically with thoughts directed toward God. However, prayer is not an incantation with magic words. God does not even hear "words." If receiving something from prayer was a matter of reciting specific words in a certain pattern, that would classify prayer as a magic spell instead of communion with God. If this was the case, through trial and error, humans would have figured out prayer thousands of years ago.

"If more rain on crops is wanted, you have to say 'please make it rain' seventeen times in a row, and it will happen." Many say they really want a husband or wife, but what they are really saying is I don't want to be alone. Or, they say they want wealth, but what they are really saying is they do not want to be poor anymore. Words do not have anything to do with it. It is the feeling behind the words that count toward harmony, and it's all about harmony, for "God looketh on the heart."

The Bible Dictionary adds, "The object of prayer is not to change the will of God." I never understood this because why else would one pray? I also thought that saying specific words opened the channel to speak to God. Both of my notions were false. Now I know that God is always with us and is not separate from us. We have constant communication with God at any given moment through our emotions. God is literally telling us what He thinks about everything we are thinking through our emotions. When we worry about anything, we feel awful, empty, and upset. Again, not because the object of our thoughts makes us feel poorly, but because we are no longer in harmony with God. Knowing something is going to go right, we bask in delicious, connective joy with God.

" *Men are, that they might have joy 2 Nephi 2:25* "

The will of God is that we have a joyful life, and God will guide us toward that state. Many mistakenly think that God has a specific plan for their life, but that would violate agency. I can attest that we have many pre-birth intentions, but they were very general. "Let me at it! I know I have guidance and will figure it out as I go along," was the feeling all around when I watched little ones coming into this mortal existence.

When we are asking

"Be not ye therefore like unto them: for your Father knoweth what things ye have need of, before ye ask him." ~Matthew 6:8.

God is not newly informed about our desires when they are expressed through ritual prayer. Desires are born and heard when experiencing all aspects of life. We are beings that are eternally becoming and wanting more: more love, more joy, more spirit, more freedom, more life. We are constantly experiencing this push toward evolution and growth. Desires are most abundantly born when someone is experiencing something undesirable. Our desires radiate to the ends of the universe.

The greatest desires are from people who are experiencing extremes of life like abusive relationships, extreme poverty, or painful bodies. These experiences plant equal and opposite seeds for loving relationships, abundance, and a healthy body. The spiritual equivalent is born in these moments: this is how, without the bad, we could not have the good. At all times, in every situation and with every thought, everyone is asking for more.

Believe that ye have received...

As I saw from the beings in the City of Light, their key to fulfilling desires was the ability to focus on harmonic similarity to the energy of what was wanted. If they wanted anything, they first imagined what it would feel like to have something–and this made their spirits soar with a delightful, heavenly confirmation. Just thinking of something began the harmonizing process. They entertained this thought on the stage of their mind, with so much stage time that soon, the object made its way to them. They tuned in to it like tuning to a radio station, and they received what they were in tune with. They became the same as their desire, and when that harmony was reached, they enjoyed the fruits of the spirit: peace, joy, excitement, and just knowing it was coming.

The people who were able to harmonize were the minority, save children. Children were innately very good at being clear on what they wanted. They seemed to know that this is how it should be. However, they began unlearning this at a very young age. Older people were always the culprit, misinforming children of "how it really was" and "why they should not get whatsoever they desired."

Certain ones were determined to keep their harmony with God and did not listen as readily but were eventually broken. Most called them the black sheep of the family.

The older people became less powerful because they sinned more, meaning they found more thoughts to focus on that separated themselves from God. While they received a myriad of painful feelings or indicators (worry, cynicism, depression, and being helpless), they would not change their thoughts because they did not think they had any power. At this point, all aspects of their life spiraled downward.

When most people want something, they feel disharmonious because they do not have it yet. They and the wanted subject are like two north sides of a magnet, never being able to come together, regardless of how much force or effort is expelled. For example, a

49

young woman who wants to find a husband has entertained countless thoughts about how it's "so hard to find a man," has concentrated on the lack thereof, and has spoken or complained to numerous friends about it that she has unknowingly repelled any potential suitors. Notwithstanding, many wonderful, harmonic matches would have crossed her path every day; however, she would never meet them due to her lack of harmony.

While I am sure I had read this scripture a dozen times before, with my experience now, it is evident these laws are not hidden:

"Therefore I say unto you, What things soever ye desire, when ye pray, believe that ye receive [them], and ye shall have [them]."
~Mark 11:24.

A more modern vernacular makes it crystal clear:

"I tell you, you can pray for anything, and if you believe that you have received it, it will be yours." ~New Living Translation (© 2007)

This is exactly how everything comes into being in every single experience. The people that radiated and basked in love and appreciation for anything would soon have that experience, in essence. They found the "feeling place" of having it, and it came into their experience. When anyone wanted or did not want something and "believed that they had received it," by entertaining the thought and becoming in peaceful harmony with it, like two magnets, they came together. It happened slowly at first, but there was a tipping point of thought where they became more practiced and comfortable with the habits, that it all came together and came fast.

> *Worry*
> *Is like praying for something*
> *You do not want.*
> *~Unknown*

In every moment, everyone that resonates with lack is drawing more of it into their lives. When people feel good and hopeful, they are on the right track to the fulfillment of all their desires. When they receive the indicator of bad or discouraged feelings, they keep the fulfillment of their desires far away and also invite more things that would similarly make them feel bad or discouraged. These are the seeds they were planting with their thoughts. So many people are accustomed to feeling bad that they could not even recognize when they were sinning–it is normal to feel frustrated, worried, and angry.

How to best receive?

> *A positive attitude causes a chain*
> *reaction of positive thoughts, events*
> *and outcomes. It is a catalyst and it*
> *sparks extraordinary results.*
> *~Wade Boggs*

You cannot receive a signal that is being broadcasted on 108 FM while tuned to any other frequency. Similarly, you cannot hear answers to prayers except while in a joyful, loving, and appreciative state. That is the frequency from which God operates and broadcasts.

Though all prayers are answered, one cannot hear the answer until they stop sinning, which means stop thinking thoughts that separate yourself from God. The problem is you cannot stop thinking certain thoughts (just try not thinking about pink elephants...). You have to start thinking new thoughts which align with God and replace the old thoughts on the stage of your mind. The first two ways are through specific types of prayer and meditation.

Through Prayers of Appreciation

> *Appreciation is the highest form of prayer, for it acknowledges the presence of good wherever you shine the light of your thankful thoughts.*
> *~ Alan Cohen*

When I saw the beings from the City of Light appreciate an object or experience, it was the fastest method for someone to become harmoniously in tune. There is a major difference in how the following two statements feel: "I want a nice house, now!" compared to "I just love and appreciate nice houses!" The lack is easily discernible in the first phrase. Appreciation is clear and pure.

Semantics aside, gratitude is different and nowhere near as powerful as appreciation or love (which are so close there is no real difference). If you think of all the things you are grateful for, you may think of all the things you have now but did not before. If you think of all the things you love and appreciate, the list becomes endless and without any negative taint. If you feel grateful for a new, reliable car, there may be a hint of negativity in remembering the old, unreliable car. It also brings back some of the incorrect Master-Servant relationships and can feel like the great, big, powerful God in the sky "gave something to little ol' me" or (as one is on their knees in devotion) "I am thankful for any crumbs tossed my way." Everyone defines things differently, and my definition of gratitude maybe your definition of appreciation. Never mind the semantics (as words have no meaning to God); make sure your thoughts are clear and pure. Your positive feelings will indicate their clarity.

Using prayer is a tool to help focus your thoughts and relax into your natural state of being. Prayer is to align your desires with God's desires. That is a good thing because God wants you to be happy, and every desire you have is because you feel that it will increase your happiness. "Whatsoever thing ye desire..." This is the true nature of the co-creative relationship. A prayer of appreciation is thinking thoughts of love and will help you get into a place where you can receive God's guidance. With all the power of focus, think and thank everything you appreciate. It may be slow at first, but as you focus your thoughts on everything you love and appreciate, more of the same will come to your mind because you start to broadcast and tune into a harmonic signal that brings more of the same to you. Use prayer to focus on all the things you love about life, and soon, you will explode with joy in your prayer. That is effective prayer.

> *If the only prayer you say in your entire life is "thank you" - that is enough.*
> *~Meister Eckhart*

And then go about your day, and seek more things to love and appreciate. It is an odd notion to literally "pray without ceasing." As vain, ritualistic prayers have no meaning or power, being in love and appreciation of all that surrounds you all day is being in harmony with God without ceasing. And your whole day will be different because you are now more harmoniously aligned with things you will appreciate when they come. You will miss out on things that make you "angry or upset" because you are not tuned to that station. If you are thinking, "easier said than done," you are correct, especially in the beginning. These are indeed how the laws work, though implementation is more of an art and a lifelong practice. Being in control of one's thoughts can be a difficult challenge. This is where meditation comes into play.

Get in Alignment with God through Meditation

> *We pay too little attention to the value of meditation, a principle of devotion... meditation is the language of the soul. It is defined as a form of private devotion, or spiritual exercise'.*
> *Meditation is a form of prayer.*
> *~David O. McKay*

Broadly speaking, meditation is the opposite of prayer–it is a focused absence of thought. The foundations of meditation come back to the basis of who we are. Jesus proclaimed that "God is Love." Since all humankind comes from God and we are like that from which we come, we are love as well. It is our natural state. As previously discussed, when we are in our original, natural state of love, we have the indicating, delicious, positive emotions of connection to God. So, in meditation, we slow down all conscious thoughts, and in the stillness is our true voice.

The voice of God is still and small over the loudness of life. Through the constant chatter of the mind, it is not often heard. So much of being who we really are is not about learning to become Christlike; it is just about ceasing those things that keep us from our natural, Christlike nature–to become as little children. Similar to an inflatable ball in a swimming pool, when we are placed deep under the water, the deeper we are, the more pressure there is. That pressure is sin or separation from God. When we let go of the hate, discouragement, doubt, and frustration, it is like letting go of the ball, and we jump back to the surface–our natural state. In meditation, it clears the thought stage of our minds. We harmonically turn off every station, and the only station left, or the default setting on the radio, is God.

How to meditate

> *Be still and know that I am.*
>
> *Psalms 46:10*

In our world of constant stimulation, meditation may not be easy for most. As David O. McKay said, it is a "spiritual exercise," and exercise is not always easy. As with all physical exercise, meditation is an incremental progression and has momentum that can become very powerful. It is not known why, but in the late 20th and early 21st century, sermons on meditation in the LDS church all but ceased, or meditation was seemingly redefined as "pondering."

Casually thinking about something is not meditation. Hopefully, readers of the future will scratch their heads at why this, one of the most powerful tools of all creation, was somewhat silenced for a season. It is possible that meditation became associated with odd behavior like monks standing on one foot in airports, beds of nails, or eastern religious practices like chanting, decade-long vows of silence, and all manner of non-meditative behavior.

In a quiet room, preferably alone, sit (or lay down if you can do so without falling asleep), relax your entire body, and focus on something simple like your breath. You can focus on each part of your body and relax it. You can count your breaths, or you can do all of the above. When the chatter begins, and your mind wanders, it will gently but firmly focus back on your breathing. Fifteen to twenty minutes is enough unless inspired otherwise. Mornings are best because your thoughts are quietest. See how long you can go without a single thought racing onto the stage of your mind. Most people cannot go for ten seconds. You will improve. Soon you will feel the power–and not only while meditating. You will also be more able to discern your emotions and thoughts throughout your day. Make it a daily practice, but never a chore. This raises your spirituality level as you will have more time attuned to God. Meditation is the heavy powerlifting in the mental gym of the mind and soul. So, when you get into real life, you will be strong and have the power to stay connected to God.

The tangible side benefits of meditation are well documented and are certainly the most beneficial activity one can do for their body. The benefits include better stress management, helping prevent heart disease, boosting the immune system, making the environment inhospitable for cancer cells to grow, and even lowering biological age. In subjects over 50 years old, some were, biologically speaking, up to 27 years younger.[13] There is a complete pharmacy in the brain, and meditation seems to dispense all of the right agents in perfect amounts. Meditation is a fountain of youth, as one may expect as a result of spending time being directly connected to God's life-flowing energy.

---

[13] Murphy, Michael; Donovan, Steven; Taylor, Eugene (1997). The Physical and Psychological Effects of Meditation: A review of Contemporary Research with a Comprehensive Bibliography 1931–1996.. Sausalito, California: Institute of Noetic Sciences. ISBN 978-0943951362.

There are side effects, though. The intangible benefits are more difficult to measure. How does one quantify a "better sense of well-being" or "better connection to God"? Scientists have confirmed that people who have practiced meditation for a few years undergo permanent changes to the core, hard wiring of their brains. When a meditator (while not in meditation) faces sudden stress, the neurological centers for anger, anxiety, alarm, and reflexive fight-or-flight do not react. For the life of the scientists and the whole scientific community, they do not know why. Could this be in fulfillment of the prophecy, "the peace that passeth all understanding?"

Meditation is not mere relaxation. Science confirms that meditators have significantly more benefits than people who have practiced mere relaxation techniques (though meditators are relaxed while meditating). This book is not about the science of meditation, nor does one need to be a long-term meditator to start receiving its benefits. However, when starting something new, it is always helpful to remember additional reasons why it is so positive for you physically and spiritually.

At the end of a long meditation, you will certainly feel a powerful peace. In this place of stillness, you are connected to God in powerful ways. This can be the time to enact Jesus' direction for receiving, "Whatsoever ye desire." Envision a situation where what you desired occurred, making it easier to "believe that ye have received, and ye shall receive." Experience all the feelings that would come as a result. This first creates it spiritually with God. You are not creating from a place of lack or to fill voids. This is the time and space where you can create "whatsoever thing ye desire" and have it come to fruition. Feel the joyful feelings as you go over this in your mind. You will adjust to the new harmony of what it would feel like to have (or become) what you want. You may also have a thought pop into your head that you know is not your own—follow it, honor it, and it will yield sweet fruits. Then, know that it has now been planted and is growing. Soon you will harvest "whatsoever ye desire." Go about your day in peace and knowing.

> *Imagination is everything.
> It is the preview of life's
> coming attractions.*
>
> *~Albert Einstein*

Studies on Prayer & Meditation

> *If you realized how powerful
> your thoughts are, you would
> never think a negative thought*
> *~ Peace Pilgrim*

There have been thousands of scientific, double-blind studies on the remote influence of prayer. Is it sacrilegious or blasphemous to "test" prayers? Is that testing God? Is that seeking a sign? Some people think so, but nonetheless, thousands have orchestrated all kinds of studies on prayer. They are indeed highly controversial, let alone when it dives into which religion has the most effective prayers. This book will not go into those specific details, primarily because of the flawed premises about God previously discussed. Christians in general, including members of the LDS Church, sometimes do not have the most effective prayers due to misunderstanding the true nature of

God and the laws. Though never spoken outright, many members believe that God actually listens to and answers Mormons' prayers more than others. This notion is, of course, false and would make God a respecter of persons. There is no religion in Heaven.

The laws have not been hidden and are throughout the scriptures. And certainly, people tried "believing that they had received," and yet, still, they did not receive. Undoubtedly, in response to these types of questions, James clarifies:

"You ask, and receive not, because you ask amiss, that you may consume it upon your lusts." ~James 4:3

Meaning that if you are not receiving, it is because something is amiss. It is not because the laws are broken, or God is saying "no" to you. Something is not in harmony. I read, "consume it upon your lusts" as "to fill voids." Also, if someone desires to kill or harm someone else, God will not assist them in this task. What they are really seeking is peace and connection to God. They mistakenly think the death of that person will bring them peace, which it will not.

As of the first part of the 21st century, studies on the intangible results of prayer and meditation remain too difficult to quantify, like increased happiness, the ability to attract a partner deliberately, and the power to create whatever you want in life. However, one of the most all-encompassing studies I found that clearly displayed the laws in action was from D.J. Benor's Healing Research. A summary of the findings follows.[14]

Leonard Laskow, an American gynecologist and healer, was recruited by American biologist, Glen Rein, to test the most effective healing strategies for inhibiting the growth of cancer cells. See if you can estimate their efficacy and whether they were harmoniously aligned with their intentions.

---

[14] D.J .Benor, Healing Research: Holistic Energy Medicine and Spirituality,vols.1-4, Researching Healing (Oxford:Helix Editions Ltd.,1993

-Imagining the cancer cells dematerializing or visualizing the condition going away.

Much was spoken concerning the "power of visualization." The result? Zero percent effective as cancer continued to grow. The reason why is that the study participants focused on what was (cancer cells) instead of what they wanted (healthy cells).

-Unconditional Acceptance

Not surprisingly, for creative beings, this is 0% effective.

-Whatever is "God's will" be done

This was about 19% effective in slowing the cancerous growth rate, but it was dependent on one's viewpoint of God. Was their version of God 'loving and kind' or 'wrathful and angry?' This tactic was not effective because it echoed back to a misconception of God–the "Master-Slave" relationship–whereas we have a co-creative relationship with God.

-Viewing the cancerous cells as normal cells

This was 39% effective in slowing down cancerous growth. It was the most effective because no thought or attention was placed on cancer, only on healthy cells. This is the "fruit" of unlocking and understanding the laws of the universe.

In 1966 the British Journal of Dermatology found that a pharmacologically incurable skin disease had a cure rate of 80% because study participants engaging in prayer and meditation saw the skin as normal. No attention was given to the unhealthy skin. What man cannot do with the arm of flesh; God can do easily when harmoniously aligned.

One of the largest studies on prayer enlisted a large group of Roman Catholics to pray for 1,800 patients going in for heart bypass surgery with the intention of "a successful surgery with no complications and a quick recovery." I have witnessed the same basic prayer or blessings given by myself and other LDS members in identical situations. As you can estimate, this was 0% effective because they were focusing on the problems (something which required medical intervention, the possibility of complications, and a quick recovery from the problem).

We know there are no positive effects to problem-focused prayers but are there any negative ones? In 1966, Dr. Scott Walker with the University of New Mexico School of Medicine studied the effects of prayer from family members toward alcohol rehabilitation participants. After rehab, the family members continued to pray for the participants to help them with their problems. After six months, Dr. Walker discovered that the group that was prayed for by family members was drinking more and was less happy than those where prayers were not being offered. This is because when family members focused on "helping those struggling with alcohol," they were focused squarely on the problem. Thus, whatever they focused on (drinking problems) expanded, and they did more harm than good. A single positive influence can be more powerful than countless negative ones when there is nothing but negative influences; hence, more damage is done than good. This is another testament that the universe does not hear your words, only the feeling behind them.

When you think negatively about someone and focus on that through the amplification of thought in prayer, your power of influence can pull that person into a worse place. The Light showed me this through the City of Light beings. Knowing this has radically changed my entire life because I realized how backward I was when approaching how to help loved ones. The whole notion of how powerful one's thoughts can be made me firmly believe what Alma proclaimed:

> "For our words will condemn us, yea, all our works will condemn us...and our thoughts will also condemn us..." ~Alma 12:14

God is not getting offended by our thoughts or bringing down his wrath upon us because we made Him feel bad. Our thoughts are separating ourselves from God, and if we plant seeds without God, we are resigned to eating the bitter fruits. Therefore, if you cannot think positively about someone because of their situation, do not think about them at all. You are doing more damage than good if you pray about someone you feel worried about. No man can serve two masters; you cannot harmonize with love and fear at the same time. The best thing you can do is focus yourself on a good feeling place and then focus your all-is-well, positive thoughts in prayer about them. You may have to start slow and move up the radio dial–finding better feeling thoughts along the way–but this is the work of positive influence.

> "A man is but the product
> of this thoughts,
> what he thinks, he becomes."
> ~Mahatma Gandhi

Jesus knew to only look at what was wanted. He insisted "thou art whole," and He knew it, and He knew it with such power and conviction that they believed it as well. It was with their faith, not magic. He did not say "be ye cured of leprosy" because that would be focusing on the problem; he focused on wholeness.

Chapter IV
Co-creating at its best

"'...He that believes on me, the works that I do shall he do also; and greater works than these shall he do..." ~ John 14:12

Now that a more perfect understanding of the nature of God has been presented (the laws of the universe and an understanding of how they tie together with your guiding emotions and the purpose of prayer and how best to pray), it is time to put them all together into creating the life you always knew was possible.

Methods of Prayer, Meditation, and Co-creation.

Prayer is co-creation with God. Is it the purest exercise of the faculties God has given us - an exercise that links these faculties with the Maker to work out the intentions He had in mind in their creation.
~ E. Stanley Jones

I was personally never satisfied with the general answer of, "you will be blessed." I always wanted the schedule of said blessings so I could do the right things that would affix what I wanted to me and my life. "Blessings" was just too vague.

I now know that it is a manner of harmony. There are two main indicators that will reveal your true harmonic thoughts on all topics: Your emotions (seeds) and your real-life created world (fruits). Both of these are mere temporary indicators. Emotions are BEFORE (seeds), and the fruit will come AFTER. Thus, it is much better to pay attention to your emotions beforehand as they indicate what seeds you are planting and tending. While you may have to eat some unwanted fruit today, adjusting your thoughts and thereby your emotions will change what fruit you will eat.

With this new awareness of thinking, being, and praying, some may attempt to do too much too soon. First, one must gain unmistakable faith in this method of co-creating with God. The following are four examples of real-life general topics. Be aware of the patterns on each topic because the pattern is always the same.

> *Do not be anxious about anything, but in every situation, by prayer and petition, with thanksgiving present your requests to God.*
> *~Philippians 4:6*

Increase Knowledge

Unfortunately, the #1 most asked question from church members in every congregation around the world is: "How can I tell if it's the Spirit and not my own thoughts?" Sometimes members would rather know exactly what to do in every part of their lives instead of figuring out the Spirit for themselves. Most do not really know if thoughts are inspired or if that voice is just the constant chatter of the mind. We want to do what is right, have the Spirit at all times, and have joyful experiences. "Following the commandments" is how we are told it is done, but it does not really work that way and makes us think we must somehow not be following correctly. This leads too many to give up or reach for void-filling substances or activities.

Confusion about what to do in certain situations may be a fruit of the way you previously lived your life. As soon as you master the laws of the universe and increase in faith and understanding, you will see new seeds of clarity being harvested. The fruits and paths will

64

become so clear that you will never doubt your way again.

"And whatsoever they shall speak when moved upon by the Holy Ghost shall be scripture, shall be the will of the Lord, shall be the mind of the Lord, shall be the word of the Lord, shall be the voice of the Lord, and the power of God unto salvation." - Doctrine and Covenants 68:4

Unless your question is, "Should I kill my neighbor and drink his blood?" you may not find answers to specific, real-world, modern problems in any scriptures today, even if it is claimed to have been written for our day. Scriptures are mostly a record of ancient peoples receiving guidance for their lives. If one can receive authoritative, level-based scripture for themselves, why even attempt to use another's? Practicing to use your own guidance is the only way to learn for oneself, by oneself.

Therefore, find "the feeling place" of having made the correct decision, knowing that an eternal being can never choose incorrectly, as there is no finality. At worst, each choice helps bring extra clarity to what type of fruits you want to harvest next. Without a diverse experience, you could never have clear or strong desires. We would literally be damned in our progression because we could not reach for more, and more is what we and this life are all about.

If there are some choices in front of you, the "bottom-line" fruit you want to harvest is to feel better. That is the root reason for all desires for eternally evolving beings. If you lead your thoughts toward elevating positive emotions, you will soon receive the right answer so clearly that you will not doubt its authenticity. One must harmonize with the thought and "feeling place" of knowing you made the right choice. Breathe a sigh of relief and know the answer is on its way. Once this feeling of peace is normal, watch for the answer–it will come soon.

Improve Health and Body

The studies on prayer and scriptures all point to the same thing: you have to create a vision of a healthy body and believe that you have it and that more improvements are coming. Does a first-time pregnant mother feel bad because she does not yet have a baby in her arms? No, she knows it is coming and does not ask the doctor to unnecessarily retrieve it sooner than is requisite. In fact, if anyone tried, she would aggressively stop them as she knows it is not the right time. It takes time for seeds to grow, and the more you notice it is not here yet, the more prolonged it will be. As if you dug up a seedling every day to check the progress, it would severely lengthen maturation, if not stop growth entirely.

That is the difficulty in creating a vision of the body you want because your body in its present "needs improvement" state seems to be with you all the time.

> *Be careful about reading health books.*
> *You may die of a misprint.*
>
> *~Mark Twain*

There are countless health, fitness, and diet books out there. If you read them all, you would be thoroughly depressed. You will find scientific, double-blind studies by credible sources that will preclude you from eating almost everything. Looking for answers with the "arm of flesh" will be a long and painful process. In fact, not being in harmony with the body you desire will guarantee that the fruits harvested will not be what is wanted.

The fact is nutritionism was debunked in the early part of the 21st century because they are not taking into account people's harmony with food or their body. Without taking into effect the laws of the universe, one will forever be searching for "the answer." Two people with the same body metrics, eating the exact same diet (one person who is stressed and eating to fill voids while another is joyful and eating to enhance their life experience), will have vastly different results or outcomes over time. In fact, consuming a cookie in joy does not cause the body's blood glucose to rise as it does in others.[15]

It is interesting to note that a cancerous growth in the body can stay the same size for years, yet upon diagnosis and informing the patient, it will explode and grow exponentially. Or when a doctor recommends a patient lose weight, the average American will gain 10 pounds in the first month because they have now added authoritative power and attention directly to the problem. Whatever you focus on (including your waist) expands.

The closest science to explaining the laws is in the placebo and nocebo effects (believing something is good or bad). However, these are difficult to measure, so scientists do not do it. At the writing of this book, 21st-century science lacks the technological capacity to measure subtle, vibrational nuances in the psyche about all topics, including food and the beliefs people hold about food. Although these frequencies are difficult or impossible with present technology to register on any scientific gauge, it does not mean they do not exist or have a powerful influence. Do not be concerned with skeptical scientists because their predecessors also did not believe germs existed until the discovery of the microscope.

If ill, when people say, "I am praying for you," if you feel so inspired, reply, "Thank you very much; however, when you pray, are you seeing me in my illness or as already recovered?" Whenever Jesus healed in person or remotely, He did not give or send healing energy to them. That would be asserting His will into another, which would violate the law of agency. Jesus knew they were already asking for a more robust body, and He only focused on seeing their balanced, healthy body. He knew it with such power that He pronounced the words, "Ye are whole," they joined right into the knowledge of their

---

[15] Zeevi, David et al. Cell , Volume 163 , Issue 5 , 1079 - 1094

wholeness themselves. Billions of unreceptive cells then relaxed their stress and came back into balance and wholeness. Then Jesus said, "Thy faith hath made thee whole" because that was true and directed, "Go thy way and tell no one." This was not because Jesus was overly humble; he knew that if the healed person went back home to his negative family, friends, and neighbors, they would convince him the healing of the "incurable disease" was false. Then he would be right back into thinking the same pattern of thought that allowed the illness to come, and it would come right back.

To become in harmony with the physical body you want, think of all the invigorating reasons why. If the reasons are "not to be overweight, not to be sick, and not to be tired" (which are all negative-based emotions), remember to focus on the positive reasons. Start wherever you are and adjust the thoughts upward until your emotions indicate joy. Words do not matter. "I don't want to be fat anymore" compared with "I love having a good feeling body and running and playing effortlessly." One enlivens the soul, and the other is depressing.

Think of all of the fun things you would do. Make lists of appreciation for your new body. When your vision makes you feel peaceful, happy, content and even excited, the work is done. The seed is planted. Then, the answer will make itself unmistakably known unto you. Someone may suddenly recommend a certain book or diet, but the difference in this diet is that God has sanctioned it for you and your body personally. With all the health books out there, each of them works differently depending on one's beliefs, body type, and philosophy. Reading and trying them all will take a lifetime and a fortune.

Let God direct a path for you. There are dozens of paths God may direct you to at any time to fulfill your every desire. You may find an exercise partner, or you may change nothing but bask in your meditative vision of how you want your body to be and watch as your body comes into harmony with your vision. You will be inspired to eat differently. Merely no longer being in harmony with non-beneficial food anymore may take you to where you want your body to be. Take no action unless it is inspired. A dreaded action is never an inspired action. Only travel on inspired pathways because they are always aligned for you personally and will always lead you to what you really want.

Create Wealth

Money is a big topic because it is so closely related to freedom which is the foundation of the universe. When you do not feel free or lack the freedom to do what you want, it is irksome on a soul level. People do not want physical money; they want the freedom that it affords. Therefore, if one can focus on freedom in one's life right now, more will come soon. Here are some gauge markers for being in harmony with financial abundance:

- You genuinely are happy for others' success (even those younger or less educated than you).
- You can give money freely (without heartache).
- You do not berate the wealthy (disharmonious).
- You do not loathe paying taxes (it is simpler to allow more into your life than change the laws).
- You do not get upset at others who "waste" money on "frivolous" things (do not we all at times? Judge ye not).
- You do not feel bad if you overpaid for something (it is okay, much more is coming).
- You are not constantly seeking "deals" to save some money (Would a billionaire do this?).
- You do not desire wealth to "help" other people (more will be written about this in Chapter 5).

I have listened to countless sermons attempting to placate why "God does not answer some prayers," giving the false doctrine of "wants versus needs." Jesus never taught, "Whatsoever thing ye desire, as long as ye really, *really* need it, and it is not just a mere want..." Whatsoever ye desire means just that. You can have anything you want in life, and what you want is more: more delight, more evolution, more spirit, more freedom, more comfort, and more fun.

69

The key is harmony.

In the City of Light, the beings who received what they wanted just felt love for nice things, even when they did not have them. They just appreciated the fact that the objects existed and loved that someone created them for the enjoyment of all. Thinking about something and feeling love for it is an indicator of perfect harmony. Those that received it never felt bad because they did not have it. The thought of having it was enough, and they enjoyed that harmony, and it came quickly into their life.

> *If wealth was the inevitable result of hard work and enterprise, every woman in Africa would be a millionaire.*
> *~George Monbiot*

Hard work is never the key factor; it is harmony with the desire which is key. Countless people are working three jobs and still cannot make things work financially. Certainly, many have harmony when they work long hours, but it was harmony and not the hard work that led to receiving. Loving what one does ensures that joyful feelings become the dominant thought on the stage of the mind in their life. Thereby, they harmonize with all things that are like unto their thoughts.

Most little children never work hard or earn money and yet receive everything they want. It is because they are clear and expectant. They know this is how the world works. The root of enthusiasm is entheos, which means having God within or to be with God. The fruits of being in harmony with God could not feel anything contrary to joy. Thus, seeking whatever makes us joyful and enthusiastic is the path from God.

Education versus Schooling

Do not feel down on yourself if you have not had what society says may be the right "schooling." "Schooling" and "education" are entirely different things. Schooling is just that; being at school while presentations are made–learning is optional. The word "educate" is from Latin, "educo" or to evoke, elicit, extract or draw out. An educated person can evoke the laws of the universe and draw out "whatsoever they desire." A well-schooled person can win trivia games but may or may not be truly educated.

It is not an "ivy-league education;" it is "ivy-league schooling." The laws of the universe do not check your credentials before delivery. Most schooling lags far behind the real world. Learn the laws of the universe in theory and in practice and become truly educated. Do not berate the well-schooled; you may need them as your faithful worker underlings one day.

"But seek ye first the kingdom of God and his righteousness, and all these things shall be added unto you." ~Matthew 6:33

Countless self-made, wealthy people, presently or in the early days of America, left schooling because they had an inner "knowing" of the laws that could not be taught. They may not have been well-schooled, but all are well-educated and very wealthy in joy and in bank statements. They all learned to harmonize with whatever they wanted, and it came into their life as a product of law. Certainly, there is more to schooling than uninspired presentations of what someone thought about something a hundred years ago. Schooling certainly is not wrong and may be requisite for certain gatekeepers of professions, but do not forget your true education.

Budgeting

Knowing the harmonic power of your words, thoughts, and intentions, one can see how the concept of "budgeting" can be a two-edged sword. Certainly, it may help maintain balance and stability. However, if more wealth is wanted than the present harmony indicates, starting out with a budget of "this is all we have each month" or "I don't have any more money after these expenses" will ensure that no more can come in. Budgeting may be the best way to financial plan for most. However, the reason you have harmonized with this book in your life is that you are not satisfied with eking out a meager existence in any aspect. You actually believe Jesus when he says, "whatsoever thing ye desire, believe that ye have received," and rather than be desireless, you will learn to master your thoughts and beliefs. So, if budgeting feels inspired to you at certain times in your life, just make sure you are in harmony with open pathways for expansion.

Tithes & Offerings

As a tool of abundance, tithing works in and out of every religion in the world. The laws are not a respecter of persons. Tithing is about feeling abundant, and giving in a manner of "I have more than enough money and can give and still have enough" is the perfect harmonic stance to do just that. Paying your tithing bitterly or resentfully negates the blessings. If you cannot get into the feeling place of abundant giving of tithing, donations, or even tips, you will never become more abundant in view of the fact that you are radiating, "I do not have enough, I lack money, and there is not enough in my life."

Give freely and abundantly, or do not give at all until you can change your thoughts to begin feeling good about it. If you do not feel like you can afford to pay your tithing, do not do it until you can feel better about it. You must feel in harmony with money while paying it. You must start from where you are at harmonically and move slowly upwards.

For example, start from a general viewpoint: "If I give this money away, I know I will not be homeless. I know my family will not starve. I have always been taken care of. Somehow, things always work out for me. Isn't it fun to have enough money that I can give away and still be stable? Money is always coming to me." Then, keep moving yourself up with thoughts that give relief from the last one until you feel abundant. It may take a minute, an hour, a week, or a month, but do the work. As always, it is the feeling behind the words and not the words themselves.

As your philosophy and feelings change about money, you will soon be inspired to paths for more joyful interactions, which will "coincidentally" bring more abundance. Then, you will see changes in your bank account. Do not try and jump up thousands of flights of stairs in a single bound. You may not change your philosophy and beliefs about money overnight. We all have well-worn, rutted thought pathways like mountain deer trails. There are pathways in the brain that are built because of habitual use. New pathways need to be created. Constructing a new road consists of extensive planning, site preparation, grading, several foundational support layers, and a myriad of other challenges along the way before cars can easily glide to their destination.

Large amounts of money are a result of being harmoniously aligned with who you really are. God is infinitely abundant and lacks nothing, and you come from God. Abundance must become a natural place in your thoughts and actions. How would someone with the wealth you desire to walk, talk, shop, and interact with others? At first, you may not want to start to spend like a millionaire, hoping that everything will turn out okay, though if you could do it, it certainly would. Imagine how you would be if you had copious amounts of money. You would feel powerful, thrilled, joyful, and natural. Therefore, these thoughts must dominate.

On the stage of your mind, this must be the foremost practiced thought until it becomes natural. Copious amounts of money must feel natural, not burdensome or overwhelming, but instinctive and logical. Your joyful feelings will confirm if your thoughts are in harmony. Uneasy, doubtful, or worried feelings indicate that you are not in harmony with abundance and need to change your thoughts.

When you are entertaining thoughts that are aligned with God, you will receive confirming, joyful feelings and evidence of the fruits of the Spirit. When you are in spirit, you can be inspired. You will receive the inspiration for a path that is in harmony with your desires. It will be so clear you will not doubt it, and nobody, including your friends or family, will be able to persuade you away from this God-given, inspired idea. If your idea sounds like a boring or painful path–that is not it. The inspired path will be a spirit and joy-filled one.

Create or Improve Relationships
Creating new relationships

There is so much push for action in the church for singles to do and not do certain things to get married. Do go to church. Do go to all of the activities. Do mingle. Do not hang out. Do date exclusively. One can spend decades preparing the garden, fertilizing it, watering it, and weeding it, but all actions are futile if spiritual creation has not yet occurred or the seeds have not been planted. So much unnecessary heartache is evident. If the relationship has not been created spiritually first or no seed planted, no amount of time working in the fields will yield any fruit, ever.

Also, with each sermon or advice focusing on the problem, countless singles say, "Thank you for yet another reminder that I am not married." The constant attention is pressure, and it is doing more harm than good because it is bringing more and more aware of what has not yet materialized. Harmonizing with "I am not married" ensures no other relationship harmony can be attained.

How many people do you know who finally gave up trying to find a partner, only to have them come into their life? It happened because they stopped harmonizing with the thought of lack. When they gave up looking, they also gave up their attention to not having. Society calls this "ironic," but it is entirely law-based, and once you understand the laws, it makes perfect sense. If you do not understand the laws or how inspiration works, you will preach advice about how life is a numbers game.

Trying to find a partner by playing the odds is the opposite of God's ways of direct, pinpoint inspiration. Playing the odds of going to 100% of all activities to find a spouse can be a long, frustrating, and circuitous path. Though when guided by inspiration, the path is short, simple, fun, and fast. There is but one thing that is needed, and that is preparing in joy.

Feel as if you were in a joyful relationship, think the thoughts until you are soaring with positive emotion, and stay in that place all day. Receiving the evidence of harmony with God through joyful feelings ensures you are now on the correct road of inspiration. So, pay attention, and you will be inspired by all things and will find a joyful relationship soon.

A joyful person will also unknowingly avoid all bad dates and relationships because they are not in harmony with them. Let the others who are harmoniously aligned with jerks date them instead. You will hear their battle cry often, "All I ever date is losers." So be it; they are always right. Never participate in any conversations about bashing the other gender. The longer you speak about something (or listen to that station), the more in harmony you are with it. Spend your time speaking, writing, and thinking about all the best parts of each person you have dated in the past or would like to in the future. Like attracts like, so when you two get together, you will have a delicious experience of two inspired, co-creating people rather than two empty people filling voids.

One must have absolute faith that while they may not yet be ready for Mr. or Mrs. Right today, the reason why they have not come yet is that God is waiting until they become more in harmony with that right person of their dreams. Work diligently at becoming the most genuinely joyful person possible so that only another truly joyful person matches your harmony. Good indicators about potential partners are their dating history. Asking about someone's "bad recent dates" is a sly way to find out who they are harmonically. If you find someone who has never had a bad date, hope that you are in harmony with someone like that.

Improving existing relationships

Did you ever have a teacher, grandparent, or other loved one who cared for you so unconditionally that you were always "perfect" around them? They brought out the best in you. You can see this with how certain children swiftly change and act differently around various adults. Did you ever have a teacher in school where nobody dared talk in their class? The instructors expected it with unspoken power that everyone in that class was very well behaved. Some of your friends expect everyone to be rude to them. If you spend a day with them, you will not be disappointed at the stream of rude people that cross your friend's path. Like attracts like.

To improve any relationship, one must turn a blind eye to all that is disharmonious (how you would not like to be treated). Spend as much time as possible thinking and writing all the good things about them and watch their personality transform before your eyes. If who they really are is indeed so disharmonious with your new expectation of your partner, they will move out from your experience–water and oil do not mix. This may sound easier said than done, and it may be painful, but everything in the universe is about harmony, and your new, clear attention to only the best parts of a partner means that a new relationship will come quickly into your experience.

Inappropriate Desires?

Is there a line between "whatsoever ye desire" and free agency? Some may think that they want to marry a specific person. They are convinced that the person is the only one in the world with whom they could be happy or possibly marry. However, what they really desire is to be happy and have a mutually delicious relationship. That is how "whatsoever ye desire" is still true.

The closest thing to an inappropriate prayer is to pray for something specific that is outside your sphere of creation. Some other inappropriate desires may include having grandchildren, a business deal with a specific person, or any void-filling activities which include hurting others or not wanting someone else to get what they want.

In essence, all that you desire is to be or have more–more love, joy, evolution, and more freedom. Our job is to tune ourselves to God and harmonize with only the best parts of life. Harmonize with everything that makes us wondrously blissful, and allow God and the laws to send us an endless parade of harmonizing delicious situations. Expect (believe that ye have received) extraordinary events so that they become commonplace. Be more surprised when something does not turn out stunningly well. That is the best way to live.

Chapter V

—————————————— The Best Ways to.... ——————————————

Broadly speaking, there is an inspired way with God and all power and a non-inspired way with man and his cleverness. It is no secret that the pattern of answers is the same (as all law-based answers are). When the laws are understood and applied so that faith is garnered, the whole universe unfolds, and all interactions become clear. The following are four examples of how to work by inspiration:

Missionary Work

I was an uninspired missionary. We systematically or "faithfully" went to every single door in an apartment or neighborhood and spoke to 100% of the people we passed on the street, hoping to get lucky with the "numbers game." Yet, knowing what I know now, if some missionaries stayed home all day to work on becoming in alignment with God and then went out when they felt inspired and talked to only one single family, they would have had complete success. Though from the outside viewpoint, being an uninspired, systematic missionary working "hard" all day appeared like we were at least faithful (though ineffective). And yet the missionaries staying home all day, becoming one with God, and only being inspired to go directly to one family per day appeared lazy and unfaithful (though effective).

Indeed, without God and trusting in the arm of flesh, so much of life is seemingly a numbers game of random events and outcomes mixed with an occasional spiritual one. Now I understand. If you want to share in the joy, you have found in anything but feel hesitation, that is God-given direction telling you that your thought is not in harmony with God's plan at this time. God is telling you that the person is not ready. Too many members think that feeling is a character defect–that if they were braver and more faithful, they would have shared the gospel message with that person. That is entirely not true. They felt hesitation because they lacked a good, God-confirming feeling. If you want to share some answers that have helped you in your life, and your friend is ready, they will ask you. If you feel inspired, it will be so easy, clear, and natural, and nothing could stop you from sharing. That is how God's guidance always feels, never with any hesitation or doubt.

It is not helpful for anyone to feel guilt (an emotion indicating the absence of the spirit or connection to God) people to "just open your mouth to everyone." The gospel has many answers, but to those that have not lived enough life to inspire the questions, the answers go beyond useless to annoying and may even be offensive. Imagine if some fervent person came up to you and said, "Excuse me, your life obviously isn't working very well..." The best missionary work is for you to master the laws of the universe and harmonize with the most delicious life imaginable. That will inspire questions from all who are around you. They will ask you, "What is your secret? How do you live such a charmed life?" If your life is full of horrible fruits, why would your non-member friends want to join you in your philosophies, ways of life, church, or anything else?

"...my ways are higher than your ways, and my thoughts than your thoughts." ~Isaiah 55:9

Is it within the possibilities of God's infinite wisdom to guide people to certain teachers, wherever they are, to help them learn unconditional love? Certainly, as it happens more often than not. Is it possible that someone who grew up in the LDS church could learn to be more judgmental of their fellow brothers and sisters rather than learn unconditional love? Certainly. Therefore, trust that other people's God-guided paths to learning, charity, and unconditional Christlike love, may not be your path. And if someone is ever noticing that someone else is not on "the right" path, then in that moment of judgment, neither are they.

"...wherefore, except men shall have charity they cannot inherit that place which thou hast prepared in the mansions of thy Father."

~*Ether 12:34*

Remember, the bar is charity, not ordinances. One certainly does not need to be Christian to have charity. Love is who God is and, therefore, who we are as well. Becoming who we really are (love) is what life's all about. The requirement of certain ordinances has been taken care of by temples. However, there is no temple saving ordinance that says, "By the power of the Melchizedek priesthood, for and behalf of so-and-so who is dead we, by proxy, pronounce a lifetime of selfless and charitable loving acts, and a Christlike heart is bestowed." It cannot be done. What Mormons have regarding eternal ordinances can, and will be, given via proxy to everyone in but a blink of the eternities. What unconditional lovers have in their hearts can, by proxy, be given to those that lack–never. Therefore, trust that God is taking care of people's pathways back to Him, and live such a fantastic life, that people cannot help but ask you for your secret. That is true inspired missionary work.

Assist others

The first step in helping others is in knowing that they do not need your help. Whomever you wish to help is already asking; it is up to them to harmonize. If you personally can "believe that ye have received" and receive, so can they. That is not an exclusive agreement you have alone with God Almighty. Universal laws work the same for everyone. However, one can be of tremendous influence to remind others of their true nature and power, just as Jesus showed us.

As the prayer and meditation studies mentioned before have confirmed, seeing another as already having received what they want is the best possible way to help genuinely. You must convince yourself so completely that when you see them in the mind's eye, they will sense it as well, with or without your physical presence. If they are in the hospital and you cannot see them as a whole, then do not visit them. At the end of your deep meditations, pick a single event that would embody the condition you desire to see in them and think it through until your vision is so clear you cannot see them as otherwise.

When the vision of your loved one is so real that your emotions are soaring with delightful relief at their recovery, this is God confirming all is in harmony and the seed is planted and well on its way to fruition. You have successfully dismissed their illness entirely from the mind. Now you have God's power with you; go and visit them. Nothing is worse than a sea of pained sympathetic expressions surrounding someone in a hospital bed. Wait until you have firm footing and can radiate their wholeness and know they will be healed with or without your presence.

The story of Jesus healing the centurion's servant is a clear example of the laws of the universe–His helping another by way of remote healing. In Matthew 8:5-13, a Roman centurion asked Jesus for help because his boy servant was ill. When offering to visit, the centurion protested and said, "Just say the word." Jesus marveled at his faith and said, "Go thy way; and as thou hast believed, so be it done unto thee. And his servant was healed in the selfsame hour." The centurion breathed a sigh of relief, so much so that it was heard throughout the universe, and with that, he let go of his worry. He changed his station from doubt and worry to faith and knowledge and influenced his loved ones to receive accordingly.

Because of free agency, one cannot force change on anyone else's "life radio dial," so they will start to receive differently. If they are tuned into illness, poverty, or loneliness, you cannot give them some of your harmony for health or riches or lend them your feeling of having a significant other. Do not be dismayed if you cannot influence another positively. They are the creator of their own life, and even Jesus could not heal people in certain towns because they had no harmony.

Helping the Poor

Interestingly enough, Jesus never said everyone should give to the poor. He said to give to the poor in a few certain situations to a few certain people to teach a point. However, Jesus did say, "For the poor always ye have with you." (John 12:8) Always? Why is that? Why cannot the poor be made into the rich? Because free agency abounds, and even Jesus cannot violate that. If people choose to plant (think) financially poor seeds, they will harvest poorly. What happens if someone rich gives their fruit to another who is poor? The fruit will be consumed unless they start to plant their own seeds of abundance.

How many lottery winners are broke after a few years? A leaky container needs to be replaced or repaired, not continually added unto. The only solution for those being in harmony with poverty is to inspire them to change their thoughts on the subject. You cannot force them to ask another for advice, learn better thoughts, or provide free books, free schooling, or anything else unless they are asking. Life inspires people to ask questions, and if they have not lived enough life yet to ask, all answers will fall on deaf, offended ears.

There was an interesting plea in an article about Africa from James Shikwati, a Kenyan expert economist, entitled, "For God's Sake, Please Stop the Aid!" He made the case that all the aid to Africa does more harm than good. Money is just like everything else in the universe; it is a tangible manifestation of intangible thought. A healthy body is the fruit of healthy thoughts. If the governments could, they would tax healthy people and give their abundant health to someone who was ill. This is what they are doing with taxing and welfare. Yet, health abundance does not operate in that manner, and it does not work with financial abundance either. If someone is bleeding steadily, you can give them some of your blood to help them along, but unless their hole is plugged or sewn up, you can give them all the blood you have until you are dead to no avail.

It is the same with money; you cannot give it to another for any long-term benefit unless the recipient changes their philosophy about money first.

Any welfare program or nonprofit charitable organization that does not begin with the basics of teaching a new philosophy is doomed for failure. And the problem with teaching is that unless someone is being asked to be taught, the teachings will fall on deaf ears. Not a single charitable effort, in the church or out, has ever had any real, long-term success without changing the philosophy of the recipient first. If the recipient does not proactively seek to improve their thoughts on the subject, life has a way of compelling them to ask so they can receive.

Here is an oversimplified example of a man in Africa who made weekly visits to a local aid center. One day, the international aid organizations stopped bringing in more aid. First, he and his friends became very angry and indignant at the "rich" West. "Why does the rich West not give to us anymore?" Eventually, all his food was gone, and he started to become hungry. Then, he noticed others in a nearby city had food and shelter. He asked once "why" and learned that he was an employee of a company. As hunger set in, he decided to work as well. He left his flock of friends and started working and associating with an entirely different flock–a flock of workers.

Instead of the philosophy of "what can I get for free," he started realizing he could work harder, smarter, and better and receive more. He may have then noticed that his boss lived in an even nicer neighborhood, had more things, and was inspired to ask, "Why?" He learns the owner has more experience and education. Now he starts to read books and continue his education about whatever subject interests him. A new philosophy starts to grow, and with that, new seeds sprout and, eventually, new fruit. After working hard for a season, he has a day off and goes back to his original flock. He offers them jobs, but they are not interested. He notices they are still complaining about the West, even though another Christian organization has swooped in with more food and aid. "Thank God!" He was accustomed to it before but now realizes they have victim mentalities. He actually cannot stand them anymore. While they will always be friends on some level, he has different feathers now and is no longer one of their flock.

In 1939 the U.S. government had programs to build massive public housing projects throughout the nation. It was to house the "less fortunate" and home the homeless. So noble, so Christian, right?

The unintended consequence was that, instead of having one low-income family in a neighborhood, it isolated all of the poor and clumped them together. Before, the low-income family in town was just that; they had less money than others. However, the poor children are still associated with the children of professionals and the working class who had successful philosophies. Now, in the housing projects, they were entirely surrounded by others with victim mentalities and with parents teaching it to their children.

Many would learn to lie, cheat, and steal as a way of life. People think they need handouts so they will prove them right. They are on welfare and know how to work the system. Being a "Good Christian" and "giving to the poor" often enables welfare recipients and victim mentalities to perpetuate through generations.

Being Christ-like empowers. As a side note, these housing projects were simple but attractive, yet within months they became run down, with trash strewn about and everything breaking down. A decade of "deferred maintenance" happened in a single year. This is what happens when you try to take the person out of the slums without taking the slums out of the person. One must change the philosophy first.

Another major reason to be careful about non-philosophy-based financial assistance is the negative effects it has on one's psyche. When you give to someone with the attitude of "here, you cannot do this by yourself so I will do it for you," it irks the soul. The "helping hands" interjects a feeling that you are poor, incapable, helpless, and not able to live your life right. Deep down inside, everyone knows they are powerful, capable beings who can figure out this life and fulfill their purpose. Giving disables and delaying them from living the life they intended. Besides, the majority (around 70% in most developed countries) of street beggars are normal middle-class people with families, mortgages, car payments, and the like. However, many are struggling with drug and alcohol problems. If you do not give to them, they may curse you now, but when they step into their natural, God-given power, they will thank you through the eternities for seeing

84

them through the eyes of God.

Another reason not to be uninspired is it is demoralizing and may even be insulting. Have you ever had someone pay for your meal at a restaurant, and you knew they were paying because they felt like you were not as well off as they were? It may have been true, but you could have paid. That does not feel good, and you may feel a little angry because they are viewing you as incapable. If people do this enough, it becomes a self-fulfilling prophecy, and they start to expect and demand it. Disabling your fellow brothers and sisters in this way is one of the worst things you can do.

So, will most non-profit organizations ever stop the horrible damage they are doing? They are not actually doing as much damage as they could because up to 99% of the donations just pay for their own salaries. The directive is not "give to the poor"; it is "help the poor." The best help you can do is stop believing they need your help, see them as they want them to be, and really live. Live such a fantastic life and radiate it out to all with whom you interact. Beam it to all that you pass on the street. See them with love and as powerful, creative, capable beings. Use the power of your mind to create whatever situation you want to see in them, so they can, for the first time, get a sense of their true power rather than the crippling, demoralizing sympathy that they receive from everyone else. That is truly helping.

Life is more of a ladder than a bed. "More" will always be the song of the eternal being of an infinite universe. Nobody will be truly happy unless they are building themselves into more. It does not take anyone more enlightened than an elementary school student after two weeks of summer vacation and watching daytime television to realize their soul is crying for more: more happiness, joy, fun, freedom, spirit, and growth.

Group Prayer

If we are all infinitely powerful and have equal ability to co-create with God, why do some people desire a group to pray for them? If someone did not understand the God-given guidance to avoid the problem they are in, what are the chances they will now suddenly be able to hear the inspiration to rise out of the problem? God has nothing to do with the changing of bitter fruit into sweet; those are the laws. God is constantly directing that person to better thoughts, which will lead to better fruits.

However, the afflicted person ignored all of the indicators up to that point. They first entertained a negative (separating or sinful) thought, and a negative feeling came as a result. Let us choose anger in this example. They ignored the indicator, then a procession of events came, one after the other, that caused them to be similarly angry as well, each bigger than the last. Finally, a debilitating illness came that made them really angry.

If you do not deal with a problem, it will get bigger and bigger until you are forced to deal with it. This is life compelling them to change or repent of the sin of separating themselves from God. It is much better to deal with a small indicator like stubbing one's toe rather than a car wreck and a broken body. Finally, their immobilized body forces them to stop and look within. They have now been 'compelled to be humble.' They may not realize how their thoughts have brought them to their present state; therefore, they now turn to others in desperation.

Though never spoken, there is a clear lack of faith when a group is asked to help pray. Here the "needy-child reluctant-parent" and "vending machine" versions of God are resurrected. Prayer is not a democratic process where it is just a matter of more votes being cast to God to "get off his cloud and act." That would not only make God a respecter of persons but kind of a jerk.

When the object of desire was granted, it was not the quantity or quality of prayer coins inserted into the vending-machine-God that caused the outcome either. In fact, as previously discussed, mass awareness and focus on the problem may have caused more damage than good. One person who can keep their eye fixed on the solution (and ignore the problem) is more powerful than tens of thousands who are praying (and concentrating) on the problem.

If the problem was solved as a result of group prayer, it was for one of two reasons: it was either that someone, somewhere in the group, found harmony with the solution powerfully enough in which they influenced the creator of the problem, or, most likely, it was the person being prayed for. They finally started hoping and believing that "with all these good people praying, God must now give it to me," relaxed their attention to the problem, and became excited about (found harmony with) how nice it would be to feel and be healed.

There is still a problem that may leave them in a worse place of having no faith in their own power and that their healing was, in fact, temporary. If they have not dealt with the original cause of the illness or problem, they would just have another experience that would make them feel angry or powerless again. It may be another illness or relapse; it may be a car wreck or some other disaster. No matter what, it will still make them feel angry or powerless. It is the law.

We have all heard people complaining, "It is just one thing after another." If they realize why they are where they are and start to change their thoughts, their life will come back into harmony with their natural state, and they will now step into their true power. That is infinitely better than exchanging this present problem for another one down the road.

Chapter VI

Philosophy as colored lenses

> *The highest possible stage in moral culture is when we recognize that we ought to control our own thoughts.*
> ~Charles Darwin

One's personal philosophy is the compilation of one's beliefs, concepts, attitudes, and perceptions of life. It is how all information is interpreted. While one's philosophy can be changed, it is not always a simple process. A compilation of over 2,000 studies was published in the 21st century about the phenomenon of people who witness an account firsthand. The topic of the study was how widely people interpret what events they claim to have witnessed. It turns out that what people say they see is actually more about who they are and, therefore, how they interpret data than what is actually seen.

These studies are not about the unreliability of eyewitnesses but the wide and varied ways of thinking and interpreting the same data, or rather, their philosophies. People standing side by side can literally see the same things but interpret them entirely differently. They have no choice in the matter; they see what they see.

For example, I used to surprise my friends' young children by picking them up by their feet, tossing them around, and hanging them upside down while I was walking around. They loved it and were thrilled by it, squealing in delight every time. They would ask for it again endlessly in typical "one more time," childlike fashion.

If certain people saw this from far off, many would smile with reminiscent joy. Others would remember how fun it was to be a kid.

However, others would just know, with every fiber of their being, that I was a horrible monster. Others may have even viewed me as a certifiable child abuser, reaching for the phone to call the police. One person's view of me may have been as an authoritarian punishing a disobedient child. Another would just "know" that I was having a bad day, was taking it out on children, and would feel empathy for me. Someone else would see me as very impatient, grabbing a squirmy uncooperative child so that we could go where we needed to go on time. They have very little thought process in the matter, for they interpret my actions how they see them. This is their knee-jerk reaction or 'reflex arc' interpretation. Like a doctor hitting a knee, there is no "trying" involved in making a knee jerk. It is a reflex. I describe a philosophy here as eyeglasses with colored lenses.

When something happens in front of a group, it is the same exact image being displayed to everyone. The same light molecules reflect off the object and travel at the speed of light to each person. However, right before the light can travel into their eyes, it passes through their lenses, where the image changes and is distorted or interpreted. Some lenses change a lot, some a little, but everyone on every topic of life in the varied aspects of health, wealth, or relationships has their own shade with every conceivable tint and differing lens prescription.

We have all had conversations with someone when you saw it "correctly," and they...did not. They were 'just wrong,' and they thought the same about you. It is not because they were wrong or you were wrong; it was because both your lenses were different. You were both actually right. You have lived a different life with different parents, read different books, prescribed different ways of thinking, watched different television shows, went to different schools of thought, and had different friends, each with their own lenses. All of these helped change the tint and prescription of your lenses on every given topic.

In a group of people watching a scene, one person can clearly be offended. Another person is wholeheartedly complimented, and yet the third person does not see anything. At first, they have no choice in the matter. They see what they see; there is no willpower about it. If you could see through their lenses, you would see the exact same thing.

It is like those magic decoder glasses in which one can only decode a hidden message while wearing the certain color decoder glasses. Someone could say they see the word "offensive," but another only sees the word "complimented." If the two swapped decoding glasses, they would see what the other was seeing. Unfortunately, changing philosophies is not as simple as swapping eyeglasses. With much explanation, one can attempt to start seeing it from a friend's point of view. Yet, even with all the explanations in the world, swapping exact lenses is not possible. It is also not a matter of just understanding their point of view. They have to adopt their point of view and ways of habitual thinking until it becomes who they are. Then, and only then, can they see more closely what the other sees.

If you sincerely desire a better philosophy and seek to do so, there will be no end to the success you will have in life. This is the single most important desire to have in life because it is in alignment with the motto of the universe: more. To see things differently is to receive different things: deeper insights, further enlightenment, larger financial means, enjoyable people, more joyful interactions, and a vibrant body. If someone appreciates everything they see around them all day, every day, they will be in complete harmony with God. A life lived with God as a constant co-creator is going to be more of an awe-inspiring life than one lived without.

One can preach endlessly about how one "should" see things differently, but unless the actual lenses are changed, no one has the agency to choose what image is seen. In the same manner, if someone looks around and all they see depresses them, they are looking at everything dis-harmoniously to the way God looks at it. Contrary to what western medicine says, it is not an antidepressant deficiency in their diet; they need a philosophical adjustment. When they change the way they look at things, the perfect pharmacy in the brain releases different chemicals that will make people feel better.

A man works on the fruits, which are just temporary, whereas God works on the seeds. Someone can certainly pretend, under the pretenses of being a "good Christian," that they do not actually see something as angering, but inwardly they are offended. They do this because they know they "should not be angry," as there are countless sermons about how one should not be angry because it is a defect of character.

However, seeing something that makes one angry is not a choice; it is just how their philosophy interprets what is experienced. There are few more annoying things in this world than someone saying being angry is a choice because it is not. Just like you cannot choose to see red when it is blue or "choose" not to be offended when someone says or does something. Yet, with some indoctrination from sermons, new books, and new friends, which will introduce new ways of thinking, eventually, one can see things differently.

Yet how exactly does one learn or teach to see things differently? In other words, how does one change their philosophy? That is the million-dollar question. Or better yet, how can you inspire others to upgrade their philosophies to one that serves them better and is in more alignment with God? That is the trillion-dollar question because if that question can be answered, every single problem in the world could be solved.

Learning how to change your personal philosophy will be covered in the next chapter.

Chapter VII

Prove me now herewith

"...and I will order all things for your good, as fast as ye are able to receive them." ~Doctrine and Covenants 111:11

God eagerly waits to direct you to "whatsoever ye desire." It has been created spiritually first and is awaiting your harmonization with it. It is not a function of convincing a vending machine God to give us our desires. Otherwise, the above scripture would read, "I will organize all things for your good if I feel like it, and if you've put in enough coins or jumped through certain hoops."

Living our lives has inspired us to ask, and all that we ask for is created spiritually first. Once harmonized with our desire, it is done and is waiting outside our very door. God stands ready to guide us straight to the door, but He cannot open it for us. It is our *ability to receive* that is the determining factor in how fast we will receive all wanted things. We are in complete control, so the goal is not to try and convince God but increase our ability to harmonize with what we want.

"...Prove me now herewith, saith the Lord of hosts..." ~Malachi 3:10

We have colored lenses that distort all we see. Several layers of tinted glass have been added to our purview as we have lived life and adopted certain ways of seeing the world. As we remove each tainted lens, we start to see a little clearer, a little brighter, and a little truer. Soon we will be able to see all things with our natural eyes, with no distortion, or through the eyes of God.

Humankind says, "change the things I look at, and I will change." God says, "Change the way you see things, and things will change." This is the time to start seeing if this is indeed how the world operates. It is time to upgrade your life philosophy so that you will see things better, plant better seeds, and start to reap sweeter fruits.

Jesus taught the purpose of fruits was to judge how one could "know them." Meaning that the quality of the fruit will tell you if the seed is good or not. If you are harvesting bitter fruits, they must come from bitter seeds, and it is time to change your thoughts. Nobody has access to your "thought garden" but you.

When something happens in your life (fruit), the first question should be, "How does this make me feel?" Whatever emotion is felt, one must admit they were feeling that way a lot recently. If you cannot admit you were the problem, then you will never be the solution, will feel powerless, and will give up on life. Or, you can look for the thought that caused the feeling indicator to activate. This is your personal harmony.

In other words, if something comes into your life that makes you feel angry, you must admit you have been feeling angry lately and will need to find out why. If something makes you jump for joy with delight, you must have been feeling joyful in that area of life; therefore, change nothing or magnify those thoughts.

Take responsibility for all creations in your life–wanted or unwanted. Those who have been trained out of listening to their soul and have been taught to disregard their emotions are at a temporary disadvantage. As their philosophy is upgraded, the emotions will become more clear and more understandable.

Either God's house is entirely law-based and is a house of order (D&C 132:8), and everything that comes into your life is affixed like fruit from seed (2 Nephi 2:10), or it is not. If it is not true, then life really is random. One would have to deal with a moody, fickle, and changeable God, and it would not matter what you did in life because someone else was in control. If the laws are true, has not your soul been tugging with delicious delight at being awakened to your true, powerful nature? Does the co-creative relationship with God speak to you on a level that makes more sense than the vending machine or genie God? Do you feel that you are meant to have an outrageously more joyful and abundant life than you are living now? Does it fill you with joy learning to plant good seeds rather than learning coping skills to deal with bitter fruits that seemingly come into your life? If so, you are a minority, and it is part of your life's purpose to be an example unto all, to show what can really be done. The following are five recommendations to best plant and harvest sweeter fruit.

Part 1: Planting new seeds:

"...I will give away all my sins to know thee..." ~Alma 22:18

One must first be willing to give away all negative beliefs and thoughts (or sins) that separate oneself from God. These are thoughts that are indicated by negative feelings such as hate, doubt, discouragement, fear, worry, sadness, blame, annoyance, etc. The list is endless. The advice to "be positive" is not because it makes you more pleasant to be around; it is to be in harmony with all positive things. The only way to rid yourself of negative indicators is to see things differently. Only then will better thoughts become automatic and will be replaced with better indicators such as joy, happiness, bliss, knowledge, power, and delight.

Parts of your philosophy may need to be upgraded. Since you cannot go back and be retaught by more enlightened parents, teachers, and church leaders, this will be your own solo journey. New ways of thinking, new ways of acting, new beliefs, new ways of being, and probably a new set of friends will all come into your life. Here is an interesting metric: if you take the average income of your five closest friends, you will find out with surprising accuracy what your approximate income may be in five years. The reason is birds of a feather flock together.

Friends are friends because they have mostly similar philosophies about life, which includes money. One may be thinking they need to find five new, rich friends. Much of that is true, but theirs and your philosophy may be incongruent at first. Similar to the odd kid who tries to fit in, not because he is a bad person, but just because the philosophies held are so incongruent, it is like trying to mix water and oil. There is little harmony.

On the thought stage of the mind, how much stage time each thought receives is of paramount importance. These suggestions are all about minimizing and eliminating stage time for anything unwanted and maximizing stage time for everything that is wanted. Though you cannot eliminate harmful thoughts (try not thinking about pink elephants), one can only replace the thought on stage with another. If you find a thought that is making you feel bad and you cannot find a better one, temporary distraction is the best way. This is the time for meditation, happy songs, television, or a game, but be careful as this is how addictions start. The same goes for helping a friend who is struggling with raising their thought level. Take them to a movie or do anything to stop that negative thought from getting a foothold. It will naturally fade with time, and then you can start the work.

Notice there is no counsel to stop "void-filling" behavior because any focus on unwanted just gives it more power. (Vow to stop eating sugar and see how long it takes before you are binging.) You do not have to sell your television and just read all day (although, if your life is horrible and you are broke, it may not be a bad idea). If you are reaching for void-filling activities and need some soul recharge, try implementing the following:

1. Stop watching or reading the news

> *The man who reads nothing at all is better educated than the nan who reads nothing but newspapers.*
> *~Thomas Jefferson*

Typical advertisement slots during the news cost more than most other shows. It is not only because more people watch the news than anything else, but because the news is 95% negative, and very interesting things happen to people's buying decisions when they feel bad. Thus, marketers eagerly relish in delight at the thought of their advertisements couched between mostly negative news stories.

A study in June 2008 in Psychological Science titled "Misery Is Not Miserly" distinguishes itself from previous research into emotional spending by explaining why sadness induces splurging. The researchers studied how watching a negative clip affects consumers. One group watched a negative clip, another group watched a positive clip, and others watched nothing or neutral clips. Then they asked the participants to be part of another "unrelated" study in which they were asked to buy or price certain things. The ones who watched the negative clip were willing to pay up to four times as much for a small item and bought a third more than the others.

The most interesting part is when asked if the previous study they participated in (watching the negative video clip) had any influence on their buying decisions, they all replied that it 100% did not–none whatsoever. Yet the results of the study cannot be disputed. The buyers were indeed influenced greatly to buy more and spend more if they felt bad first.

This is the whole point of the news, nothing more. When news claims to be "fair, balanced, and accurate" with the slogan "This is your world today," this is a lie. When you harmonize with a lie, you will always feel bad and seek to fix the bad feeling by either finding a better thought to focus on or reaching for something to fill the void.

"...If there is anything virtuous, lovely, or of good report or praiseworthy, we seek after these things..." ~Thirteenth Article of Faith

As far as ratings go, fewer people in the history of television watch the news now because it is so negative, and not everyone is blind to their connection to God. In America in the early 21st century, an outcry from viewers about the news' negative bias was rebutted by a major news network. They retorted that there were not very many positive news stories. They even asked viewers to submit stories that were positive, newsworthy, and uplifting. Viewers submitted so many stories that it crashed their servers. What was the outcome of all of these tens of thousands of positive, uplifting newsworthy stories they collected? Nothing, and it was never spoken of again. News marketing executives know that without negativity, sales drop, and advertisers will go elsewhere.

Unfortunately for news marketers in the United States, violent crime has declined single and double-digit numbers every year since 1994. Their solution: search farther and wider for more negative stories since crime continues to lower. The reporting of violent crime has actually increased in reverse proportions to crime trends. For example, while murder has gone down by over 50%, the reporting of murders has risen over 1,600%. When crime peaked, you may have heard three violent crime-related stories. At the time of writing this book, they should only report one but are now reporting over 30 stories.

That is not "fair and accurate reporting." Those are lies designed to do one thing: create a void so viewers will buy more stuff in the hope of making that bad feeling go away. If you feel bad long enough and listen to the lies the news spews long enough, you will get so disconnected from the health that is naturally yours that an illness may come. Harmonize with that uneasy feeling long enough, and that dis-ease will yield the fruits that are in line with the disease. Typically, the news has its primary sponsors to help with diseases too. However, it is not an unusual coincidence for there to be an alliance between the news and pharmaceutical companies in the United States (one of the only countries in the world where this is legally permissible).

After God created the world, He called it "very good." This approval has not been revoked, and someone trying to convince you otherwise is not in harmony with God. Is it any wonder that those who willingly sit for an hour or two each day listening to the "truth" about the world's status would be the most negative and diseased group in the population? It has been said that the best lie is 99% truth. When someone is trying to convince you that the news (while depicting technically true events) is an accurate representation of what is happening in the world, that is the biggest lie of all. Just think, if someone traveled the globe for a year versus someone who watched a 24-hour news agency, who would have a more accurate representation of the world?

If something apocalyptic happens, someone will tell you. Otherwise, enjoy the silence and have pride in your ignorance about what is happening to 0.000000001% of the population. The world is overwhelmingly positive and bright. The positive interaction outweighs the negative one million to one. Many people take pride in being "well informed" by reading newspapers and news magazines and learning from television what is happening in "the world," what they should be worried about, or whom they should hate. Being aware of what is occurring to a fraction of the population is not an accurate representation of world happenings and is grossly, embarrassingly, misinformed. That is what Thomas Jefferson was saying.

2. Start to meditate daily

Starting to meditate will fulfill the prophecy, "peace that surpasseth all understanding," and improve every single aspect of your health and life. It will not remove all of the world's bumpy roads (which can be fun if you have the right philosophy) but will give you shock absorbers.

In the early 21st century, countless scientific studies have confirmed that stress is the cause of between 80-95% of all diseases. If stress is the catalyst, then deep, meditative relaxation may be curative. Unfortunately, this cure will not be propagated as few can become wealthy selling the benefits of meditation. Besides the personal benefits to one's body and soul, there seems to be a powerful, unintended consequence to those who also surround meditators.

In Washington, D.C., a demonstration about the positive effects that meditators can have on crime rates was conducted. There seemed to be a tipping point when the experienced meditators reached a threshold of 1% of the population. When a group of imported, long-term meditators reached 1% of the population in D.C., a corresponding drop in violent crime was found, around 24%[16]. This was maintained for several months to ensure no other factor was at play. When the meditators left, the crime increased back to normal levels. Before the study, the police chief said the only way a crime rate would drop that much was if four feet of snow fell on the city in the summer. He is now a fervent believer.

Similar studies were duplicated in 24 U.S. cities where experienced meditators (making up only 1% of the population) meditated to reduce crime. The crime rate dropped again by about one quarter in each of these cities. In an additional follow-up study of the 24 cities when a threshold of 1% of the population as experienced meditators was reached, the cities experienced an average 22% decrease in crime and 89% reduction in the crime trend.[17]

A different group of meditators aimed at the Palestine conflict

[16] J.Hagelin,etal.,"Effects of group practice of the Transcendental Meditation program on preventing violent crime in Washington ,D.C.:Results of the National Demonstration Project, June-July 1993,"Social Indicators Research,1999;47(2):153-201.

[17] M.C.Dillbeck,etal.,"Th eTranscendental Meditation program and crime rate change in a sample of 48 cities, "Journal of Crime and Justice,1981;4:25-45.

in 1983. During their sessions, they made daily comparisons between the number of meditators working on the project and the state of Arab and Israeli relations. On the days with a high number of meditators, fatalities in Lebanon fell by 76%[18]. Their reach apparently extended beyond the arms of the conflict, as ordinary local violent crime, traffic accidents, and house fires also decreased.

When skeptical statisticians worked on the probability of these events, it was calculated to be less than one chance in 500,000,000 or two in a billion. That is commonly referred to as zero, which means that it was certainly caused by the meditators and no other factor. However, scientists still do not have the equipment sensitive enough to discover what these meditators are doing. It continues to "surpass[eth] all understanding." However, they seem to be calling down heavenly peace, like Jesus raising the spirituality of all who surrounded him. Meditators are calling down and broadcasting heaven out to all who surround them. I cannot help but think that members of the LDS faith are over 1% of the population of America today. I wonder what kind of peace on earth we could help usher in if we were to join the meditators in droves. Should we not all be actively engaged in a good cause? What is a better cause than world peace?

3. The best books

"...seek ye out of the best books words of wisdom, seek learning even by study and also by faith." ~Doctrine and Covenants 109:7

Notice it does not say, "occasionally seek" or "if there is nothing good on television, seek ye..." This is one of the best ways to help change your philosophy if you were not raised or are not already surrounded by people who are successful in every way imaginable. The problem with trying to find a new flock that is more suited to you is you. You may want to think like an eagle, but you have been raised

---

[18] W.Orme-Johnson, etal.,"International peace project in the Middle East : The effects of the Maharishi technology of the unified field" Journal of Conflict Resolution,1988;32: 776-812

by chickens and think like one. Eagles do not like to hang out with chickens, not because eagles dislike or are better than chickens–their worlds are just too different, and they would not have harmony. However, with free agency you can learn to think like an eagle as they often write books about how they changed from thinking like chickens into eagles.

We all desire to give a respite to our minds sometimes. Einstein would play the violin to give the left side of his brain a break. Most today choose to try to fill voids by watching television or playing games. Certainly, there can be the same escapism in reading as well. However, at the end of watching a thousand hours of ball games, you will be no better than before. Yet, after reading a dozen of the best life-changing books, you can be an entirely different and better person. Seek an escapism activity that improves who you are and feeds your soul, like reading the best books.

Choosing what books to read

> " *The soul becomes dyed*
> *with the color of its thoughts.*
>
> *~Marcus Aurelius* "

If you intend to improve your philosophy of life, it is as simple as "seek, and ye shall find." Harmonize with how you want your life to feel, fill your life up with all kinds of "the best books" that you feel inspired to read, and dive right in.

Have you ever noticed that every house over a million dollars has a library filled with books? Does that make you curious? There is a reason for it. You will notice a large selection of philosophy books in each library. They will not be books on how to get-rich-quick or invest-money-in-real-estate schemes; they will be books dedicated to how to think or how great people thought. If you want to improve in any category of life, find people you deem successful in that particular area and ask them what books they would recommend. Write them letters if you do not know them personally. Then read all of the books that they recommend and which you feel inspired to read.

Also, in your inspired seeking, read all books that the universe crosses with your path in a deliberate way. However, reading books like these can be difficult, just like using someone else's eyeglasses (philosophy) to see, because that is what you are doing when you pick up a book and read it: you are looking through someone else's glasses for a time. It can be very uncomfortable, even painful, as many of these authors have prescriptions that are very different from yours. Also, many of these books will eliminate some of your favorite excuses as to why your life is not going well. You may hate it so much that you may throw the book across the room, literally or figuratively. That is a good sign. If you have never even desired to throw a book, you have probably never been challenged. Sometimes, you may have to stop reading the book and continue reading other books. Come back to the book in six months, and you may find that then, it may be the best book you have ever read. This means you have been growing and evolving in the past half-year.

Historical and current non-fiction, best-selling book lists can be pearls of great price. But do you really care to read what the masses are reading? I thought the same thing. I was wrong. At the time of this writing, most Americans do not read books. So, the ones who are buying and reading the books are the leaders in America. Here are some interesting facts about the lack of reading:

- The number of people who will not read past the first chapter: 60-98% depending on the book.
- 54% of people never read another nonfiction book outside of school for the rest of their lives.
- The National Endowment for the Arts report titled "Reading at Risk" found only 57% of American adults claimed to have read a book in 2002. This figure is most likely inflated.
- The average Fortune 500 CEO reads 4 to 5 books per month. (That is a few hundred times more than the average American. "Coincidentally," they also make a few hundred times more incomes than the average American.)

> *Great minds discuss ideas,*
> *average minds discuss events,*
> *small minds discuss people.*
>
> *~Eleanor Roosevelt*

T7hough it is disputed that Eleanor Roosevelt actually said the above quote, it is a very interesting thought. If you want to change your philosophy, you will usually not find it in books about events, historical or current, or magazines about people. Also, most textbooks and fictional books are devoid of life-changing philosophy. Certainly, there are countless exceptions; however, you want the "idea books"- the best-selling, nonfiction book lists.

In the field of non-fiction, if all of the current or historical events, auto/biographies, and academic and technical how-to books are taken away, there are few other categories but philosophy, self-help, and spirituality. These are books about changing one's philosophy. Self-help is a world apart from books that help shape a better philosophy, though they are often categorized into one. Most of the advice given is straight-up "self-help," a "there-there, life is random and hard, and it will all be okay in the end, I promise" type of books that are of little value to changing philosophies. Stories about how people dug themselves out of holes that they dug themselves into may be inspiring, but they are often not the philosophies that should be emulated.

What life-changing books would I suggest?

Some ideas and philosophies are infinitely advantageous for everyone to adopt. However, directing you to me or someone else's path is the antithesis of this book. You have inner direction. Let life inspire answers which will be infinitely better and more satisfying than anything I or anyone else could give you. Believe that "ye have received" and then wait for the inspiration to ask someone about their favorite life-changing books or do an inspired search for books yourself. It is one of the least threatening questions you can ask anyone and yet the most insightful. I have never met a successful person who did not have dozens of book suggestions for me. I have also never met a single unsuccessful person who could recommend any life-changing books–though they could tell me their favorite movie and television show. Read into that however you like.

More convenient education through technology

It can often be difficult to find time to read. Luckily, technology is readily making it more convenient to read books on audio. If you have a long commute and a desire for a better philosophy, you have a big advantage over those who do not. Purchase a digital audio player for your vehicle or person, no matter the financial cost. It is time to change all your travel time into time invested in your education. I am certain, without question, that turning travel time into reading time will have a more profound effect on one's education than attending a university course anywhere in the world.

You will also start to love congested traffic as it will give you more time to sup from delicious wisdom from the greatest minds of the world. If you have the discipline, e-readers may help as well. Just ponder the world's great thinkers writing down all of their wisdom into a book. You can obtain a lifetime's worth of wisdom in a few hours from a single book. Books are the most undervalued object in the world. A single book can make your fortune in wealth, happiness, and life.

But... I cannot listen to books; I cannot pay attention

When you are listening to your friends in the car, do you ever hold up your hands and start waving for them to stop? "I can't listen to you talk; I need to read the transcript of what you're saying." Of course not, because you are focused, paying attention, and are following along with zero effort. You are interested. Besides harmonizing with what you do not want (poor listening skills), you are slowing your evolution with a negative, self-limiting belief that says you cannot listen to books. To claim you can listen to someone talking is confirmation that you do have the ability. Listening skills are just like everything else; they are a muscle that needs to be used. If you need to get started with mental candy, find a few excellent thrillers to read and help train your mind to listen for the meat that is to come.

4. Disassociate with all negative and misinformed groups

> *The secret of change is to focus all of your energy, not on the fighting the old, but on the building the new.*
> ~Socrates

With an understanding of the laws and the power of focusing, fighting against any problem has a counterintuitive effect; the problem just becomes more. This is why Jesus said, "resist not evil," meaning do not give it any attention. "Turn the other cheek," meaning no matter what, do not face or fight against unwanted things. Any support group for a problem needs to be carefully scrutinized and see if they are problem or solution-focused.

Do you find it odd that the only successful effort that has ever significantly reduced any crime rates in a short amount of time was a tiny army of meditators? All the politicians and police in over 200 years of American history with trillions of dollars and millions in workforce have never been able to do what 1% of the population did indoors, with their eyes closed. It is true that the power of the few with

God is more powerful than millions using the 'arm of flesh.' For some unknown reason, the criminals just did not feel like committing crimes anymore, or the people were not in harmony with being victims.

We also need to look at the reasons behind the thought of "becoming involved in politics." Do we want to become involved in politics because it is a futile and dirty game that needs more good people? Or do we get involved in politics because the real reason is so we can be part of positive change? If we can skip getting involved in dirty politics and just go straight to helping create real change, should we? There are countless hours spent arguing, listening, watching, and reading about politicians that claim they can improve the quality of people's lives. However, if the people spend that same amount of time improving themselves, they would have the life improvements that the politicians are endlessly promising and not delivering.

Politicians have no power to plant seeds in your garden, as that would violate free agency. (That was the devil's plan, he knew the unchangeable laws as well, and he was going to force us to plant the right seeds so we could yield the right fruits.) One can certainly be worried that politicians are going to do something harmful to them, but with that worried outlook on life, politicians are the smallest problem they have. One in meditation (with God), focused on the solution, is more powerful than all of the politicians joined with all of their supporters who are focused on a problem.

Many Christians, LDS included, are sort of waiting for Jesus to come and kill all the "bad people" and usher in world peace. That is not how it is going to happen. We are going to have to participate. Whether He comes in your lifetime or not, do you want to be actively engaged in bringing about world peace or sitting on your couch waiting for someone else to start it? What excuse would you give for not spending your life working to spread peace and love on earth? With no excuses, politely pardon yourself from any group, activity, or party you are a member of that is not in harmony with God and His ways.

5. Harmonize yourself with God at all times, not just in prayer

There is a power in physically writing down long lists of all the things beloved and appreciated by you. Purchase a small, pocketable empty book and start writing. True, it takes longer to write it than to type it. And that is the point, as it is all about the amount of time you are focused on being in harmony with God. Do not worry about duplicates. Whatever you love and appreciate at the moment, write it down. That amount of stage time on the mind will echo and reverberate throughout your whole life. Carry it with you always for a time and use it often. It will slowly tune you into being in harmony with more things to appreciate. You will know when you are successfully harmonizing when in the middle of all your normal thoughts in the day, you find yourself discovering more things you can write down in your book. Like attracts like. Make this a habit. It usually only takes about three weeks to imprint a habit upon the brain.

After you are feeling ecstatic and so very blessed, this is the time to pray and express heartfelt joyful prayers of appreciation and love for God and all that is in this life. Your spirit will sing and soar as you harmonize with God through love and appreciation. Know that God knows all that you desire and is organizing your rendezvous with something that will make you want to sing and soar with appreciation. It is the law.

Part 2 - Harvesting new Fruit:

Miracles do not, in fact, break the laws of nature.
~C.S. Lewis

As you harmonize with all lovely things and start to see life through the eyes of God, your whole world will change. It will actually feel and seem like a new earth. Your life will start to spiral upwards into better and better everything. You will start to understand, with perfection, all interactions of life and know where you need to make adjustments. You will be able to see how people rendezvoused with their current situation and what other people will rendezvous with in the future if they do not change their harmony.

In 1988 President Ezra Taft Benson echoed this principle: "Yes, men and women who turn their lives over to God will discover that He can make a lot more out of their lives than they can. He will deepen their joys, expand their vision, quicken their minds, strengthen their muscles, lift their spirits, multiply their blessings, increase their opportunities, comfort their souls, raise up friends, and pour out peace." This is exactly what life is like, co-creating with God as you intended.

As you fill your life full of appreciation for all things, you will no longer desire many of the things you thought you wanted. This is an indication that much of what you desired was to fill the voids of your soul. With no voids to fill and appreciation and love abounding, a new parade of amazing and wonderful things will come into your life, even things that you formerly wanted but no longer felt the desperate need for. As you may casually appreciate things, you will find them coming to you easily and without effort because of your perfect harmony. Are you aware of any actor or actress that is popular, wealthy, and famous - yet they are not attractive, talented, or unique? It is because they are in harmony with their desires, and nothing else matters.

Jesus said, "Be ye wise as serpents." This is because snakes can shed their old skin entirely. We can be wise and discard our old negative, poor, victim mentality selves as well and become a new being. Others will think you are magic, and in a way, you are because you are co-creating with God. As intended.

109

You will notice your health is improving as you are being inspired to eat better and move your body more. Also, the voids that you previously filled with junk food no longer exist. You will no longer care about what the government is doing as you know you have more power than they could even imagine. Harmonizing with more wealth is simpler than trying to force hundreds of politicians, thousands of miles away, to change countless laws that may fractionally impact your life.

Relationships may take a shuffle as people who are no longer in harmony with your newer positive ways of thinking will feel uncomfortable around you and vice versa. You will always love them, and you may reunite again if you or life can inspire them to become more, but now you will find that you are unwilling to participate in certain negative conversations. More friends will come. (Someone said it is lonely at the top. It most certainly is not; it is just less crowded.) Basically, the scripture will be fulfilled:

"...all things shall work together for your good."

~Doctrine and Covenants 90:24

Not everyone is destined for the greatness you seek. I will never understand why, but some are just content as they are. There is no shame in that. No extraordinary efforts are to be attempted to raise them up unless they are asking. Be a compelling example, and wait for the questions.

Be appreciative of little annoyances; they are just indicators to raise your thought awareness and pay more attention. Little annoying things are a sign that you have been entertaining little annoying things on the stage of your mind. Be appreciative that your guidance and connection with God is working, and find the culprit thought. Work your thoughts into a better place. It is much better to stub the toe and change your thoughts than ignore all the other indicators, which may result in a much more dramatic manifestation.

"As to trials, why bless your hearts, the man or woman who enjoys the spirit of our religion has no trials; but the man or woman who tries to live according to the Gospel of the Son of God, and at the same time clings to the spirit of the world, has trials and sorrows acute and keen, and that, too, continually."
~Brigham Young

That certainly describes many people's lives. Countless Mormons pride themselves on their "trials." As if they are more worthy of being tested or believe that perhaps the devil has targeted them. With knowledge of the true nature of God and the laws of the universe, you can see the truth in Brigham's statement. Someone that was living according to the Gospel of the Son of God would be connected and guided. Compelling trials are absent to beings that are compelling themselves and cocreating only sweet fruits with God.

Your Beginning

I know that only a fraction of the population will be in harmony with this book. It answers questions that, if never asked, will fall on deaf ears at least and be annoying or disconcerting at best. There is no shame if no harmony is found in these words. If harmony is found, the thoughts resonate with you on a level that you cannot deny, and you will find the ideas sticky, turning over in your mind, and difficult to dismiss. As you come to an understanding of these laws, you will soon see evidence of your improved life, beginning with better feelings indicating more harmony with God.

If you can be at peace and know that your new, improved life is coming, never dig up your plant to see the progress; soon, all improvements will show up. And your family and friends will beg to know your secret and how you became magical in your life. We are literally kindred spirits, from a small spiritual family to be an example to all of what can be done.

Therefore, seek joy (not mere pleasures or distractions.) Seek reasons to laugh, play, praise, and uplift others and yourself. Seek out the beauty in people, in nature, and in yourself. Seek for something in every part of your life that brings a reason to love. Love is who you really are; it is your natural state. It indicates you and your Heavenly Father are one in those moments. Spend as much of your life in those moments, and fill your life as full of this harmony as possible. In love, you will be guided in all things to the most fruitful, joyful paths of life. Your life will spiral ever upwards. Enthusiastically following your bliss creates harmony with God that will bring more abundant life to support 'whatsoever ye desire.' The whole purpose of life is joy and to unabashedly be who you are, with no apologies. Greater things shall you now do.

Appendix
— What about... —

1. ....Job of the Old Testament?

Job is the oldest book in the Bible. The premise of Job never sits well with most, as if God and the Devil are hanging around playing a game of one-upmanship, looking for someone to torment or test (God does not test man–James 1:13). It is my personal opinion that much of the Old Testament was not necessarily from God in all the fullness of truth but was given to a certain people, with a certain level of understanding, to teach through storytelling rather than an accurate historical accounting. I, along with most, can also never get in harmony with the antagonistic personality or "Old Testament" God. The Book of Job is most certainly more of an allegory than documented fact, as this story teaches one of the most important, all-encompassing lessons of the entire Old Testament. With a little light, the parable of Job teaches about the nature of God, the purpose of commandments, what sin is, forgiveness, the purpose of repentance, and how things are invited into your life.

We know God is not a conditional lover, meaning, He does not need to require certain conditions to radiate or be loved. We also know that God has an eternal perspective to see the good in all things ("All things are for thy good"), and God can see the true side of everything. Just as a parent can see the value in the stumble of a toddler finding their balance. We know that God wants us to be happy, yet why are there commandments telling us not to do certain things? We know that we are not so much punished for our sins but by our sins. Breaking the commandments will not make us happy, and God has a vested interest in our happiness. We also know the law of the harvest, like attracts like. Sinning puts one on a path that will not take them to happy destinations. When we sin, we tune out ourselves from God, and we can no longer hear God's guidance. It is as if God is broadcasting on 108 FM, and we have moved down to 106FM; no matter how hard we listen or how much we turn up the volume, we cannot hear Him anymore. If you are high on cocaine or on a murderous, hateful rampage while God is talking to you, you cannot hear Him; you are operating on a frequency that is not in tune with God. God never changes His broadcast station; we have to move up to converse with Him. The good thing; it is the default station on the radio.

Ponder this scripture from Revelation 21 talking about those who will have a part in the second death:

"...Unbelieving, abominable, murderers, whoremongers, sorcerers, idolaters, all liars..."

Above is a list of the largest sins one may commit. These are the things that, if committed, will separate you from God more than any other act. However, I removed one of the gravest sins from the scripture list. Can you guess which sin I left out? It is a sin that has been echoed down from every modern prophet to date. The very first sin on the list is: Fear. Fear is a sin? A big sin? Yes, the biggest. "For God hath not given us the spirit of fear, but of power, and of love, and of a sound mind." It is not that God gets offended if you are fearful; it is just that if you are fearful, you are separated from God. (One can never be totally separated from God, but this is about as far as one can get.) The opposite of love is not hate, it is fear. Fear is the antithesis of love, and thus, there is no more emotion that is further away from God than fear. Also, since the law of the harvest is still in effect, the reason why God warns against being in fear is you are then on a pathway that is not in God's light and will lead you to places that you do not want to go. We know that all things were created spiritually first. Not even the devil has any power as "the devil has no power over you unless you allow it."

We also know the purpose of fruits, according to Jesus, is how "ye may know them." It is how you can judge things. If a seed, a person, or a thought were good, it would yield good fruits. The fruit is just a way to tell what seeds you have been planting (or recently thinking). Fruits are not a final judgment because more are being planted,

114

grown, and harvested all the time. That bad feeling is telling you that the thought you are thinking is not aligned with God (and you may desire to change it). If you do not change your thoughts away from depression or hopelessness, they will get bigger and bigger and bigger, and if you keep ignoring them–keep harmonizing there–you will get a manifestation that will make you feel similarly: powerless and depressed. This is how it is being punished by your sins.

Back to Job, we know that all of Job's friends begged him to just "curse God and die," but he held out. Wasn't he faithful? However, what was Job repenting of in Job 42:6? "Therefore, I despise myself and repent in dust and ashes." Was he not faithful? Did we miss a sin somewhere? Let us go earlier in the book of Job and see:

"For the thing which I greatly FEARED is come upon me, and that which I was AFRAID of is come unto me." ~Job 3:25.

Job was worried and scared that he would lose all he had. He was harmonizing with the thought of loss and was receiving the indicator of bad, gut-wrenching fear. Meaning he was not in harmony with God. Job created his loss himself by his thoughts about losing it all. He then received the indicator of fear which was God telling him to change his thoughts; otherwise, the laws were going to get a hold of him, and the fruit of loss would materialize. Most lessons about Job are about how life can be horrible and random, and those bad things can come into anyone's life–even one as faithful as Job. It also teaches how one should be appreciative because their life is not as horrible as Jobs'. Notwithstanding, deep lessons about understanding the laws also reside within this tale. The story of Job has a hidden analogy that is available only for teachers. It solves the unsavory mystery that God and the Devil hang around, shooting the breeze and looking for something to do or someone to test and torment. They are not playing with us–that would violate free agency. Nobody has the power to affect your life, especially the devil, without an invitation of thought. Nothing can have power over you.

2. ...events like 9/11?

If certain people are not in harmony with disasters, they will not rendezvous with them. Something will always happen which will cause them to be elsewhere. There are no "near misses" as a watermelon seed never narrowly misses becoming an oak tree. It is the law. With this in mind, I find it interesting that each of the four planes involved in the terrorist attack on 9/11 had about half the people that they typically did for the same time/date/flights (51.3% and 31.4% aggregate). So, one morning, four planes, and just those four planes, for "some reason," had about half the passengers they usually did. Indeed, these four flights were typically lower passenger-filled flights[19], but on that day, they were all half as full as they usually were.[20] Statistically, it is true that one plane could be explained. Two, however, cannot. Three flights are not even within the realm of real numbers, and four is so astronomically beyond all explainable probabilities that something metaphysical is certainly going on here. There sure were a lot of "lucky" people that day. Again, about half of the people who were supposed to be in the Twin Towers were not as well. Similar evidence was found about train crashes in the 1950's. Certainly, there is no death (as we are all eternal beings), and I can't help but jump with joy inside whenever I hear about anyone's "death," regardless of how they died. However, some people were more in harmony with life than death. They felt inspired, or something else came up that kept them from the vicinity of the disaster. In interviews, nobody who missed their flights or who did not go to work on time that day had a "bad feeling" because that is not how your inner guidance works (contrary to how I was taught growing up). What feels true: A loving God guiding people where to go for the best fruits of life? Or a God who constantly informs people of bad things that are on the way? If God is all-powerful and all-knowing, would it not be better for God to inspire someone towards a delicious life? God is about life and joy, not just avoiding the worst parts of life. That would make God

---

[19] Pfaff, William. 2001. "International Herald Tribune" New York. September 12, 2001.

[20] Targ, Russell. 2012. The Reality of ESP: A Physicist's Proof of Psychic Abilities. Quest Books.

powerless, void of agency, and violate the laws of the harvest. Basically speaking, unwanted circumstances and events will not allow anyone who is not in harmony with them to join in.

Consequently, one does not need to be fearful about unwanted things. Just remember to stay in a harmonious place and be open to any and all guidance. When inspired to do something else, do not rebut with, "but I always/am supposed to do _____." Go with the flow; follow your God-directed path. Someone cuts you off in traffic? Bless them. Everyone that has been in an auto accident has pondered that if they were only 2 seconds faster or slower, they would have avoided the entire event. In a very real way, this is God guiding you around unwanted events down the road. God wasn't working overtime on 9/11; he is working in people's lives all day, every day, to those that listen. Apparently, about half do. In a very real way, all kinds of things (you complain about) are God's ways of directing you toward what you really want. Be open to being inspired to alternative pathways.

It reminded me of a 2008 poll that was conducted by a major news network. The readers were asked, "Would you vote for a Mormon president?" Most Mormons believed that between 70-95% of Americans would answer "No." In reality, 94% of about 200,000 respondents said that they would indeed vote for a Mormon president. This means that the vast majority of Americans have no problem with Mormons and would even vote and support said person if they agreed with their political philosophy. Continuing to teach about hundred-year-old oppression, constantly reminding members of past hardships, injustices, pains, trials, and struggles, only harmonizes those thoughts to one's present life.

Teaching fear is not God's plan. Seeds planted in harmony with those thoughts will yield bitter fruit. Teaching a philosophy that Mormons are still hated provides an opposite view of how the world really is. This is another reason why people are afraid to share the gospel; they have a totally inaccurate viewpoint of how others view us. Never speak or teach to others anything that you do not want, essentially more of in your life. Mere focus on something starts to create harmony with it. It is time to put the past to rest.

3. ...bad things happening to little children?

This topic is a difficult one. It is an unspoken thought that babies know nothing, are basically ignorant and unenlightened, and cannot harmonize with anything wanted or unwanted because they are nonverbal. "Tabula Rasa" is a phrase meaning "blank slate" and is the most popular notion of how people come into the world. Nothing could be further from the truth. (Jesus was right about the little children, and I can certainly agree that the best advice in the world is still 'be like little children.')

First of all, many come into this world intending to be teachers, to be examples to all of what can be done, regardless of circumstance. This is their pre-birth intention. To be a teacher, one must have answers. To know the answers, one must have had life inspire the questions. To have the questions, one must have had a lot of undesirable things happen to inspire the asking. Having these experiences will enable one to help in the teaching of others by example because they really know what others are going through.

Secondly, children so quickly adopt their parents' harmonies to all things. If parents are incessantly worried about their children, just like in the prayer studies, they are doing them more harm than good. Worry, or fear, is the antithesis of God. Surrounding a young child with feelings opposite of God is inviting all kinds of unwanted experiences. I saw, without exception, that The Light and the beings in the City of Light, the most worried parents (the ones that sin the most or hold thoughts that separated them the most from God), had children with all kinds of problems: countless allergies, health problems, behavioral problems, developmental delays, countless injuries, and rare diseases. Studies on adopted children have shown how quickly a child's health can change from weekly visits to the hospital to zero visits a year–all due to one's parental philosophies and the harmony of each parent that surrounds the child. I realize this is not popular, as blame feels better than guilt, but people need to accept their personal responsibility for the thoughts they hold. "Yea, our very thoughts will condemn us." (Alma 12:14)

4. .... Satan?

If you pick up any manual, there are no lessons on the devil. We, rightly so, pay and give no attention, and therefore we give no power to Satan. In the City of Light beings, I saw that most of what people thought of as the presence of evil was just the absence of good or God. Satan has so little power. In fact, the Prophet Joseph Smith clarified that Satan has "no power unless you let him." So more accurately, before people say, "Satan tempted me, and I overcame, "they should say, "I allowed Satan in, he beat me up, and then I kicked him out." Who is better, those that do not allow satan in, or those that allow satan in and then somehow overcome him?

When people felt "tempted," this was because they were sinning, meaning they were thinking a thought that separated themselves from God. For instance, they felt they were inadequate, and God did not agree, and they felt the absence of God; they felt bad. In this bad feeling, they reached for a void-filling activity to try and make the pain go away or at least not be at the forefront of their mind. Have you noticed that if you feel horrible, you eat horribly? It is because you are in harmony with those horrible substances; it is not because you are "tempted by the devil."

I pity those at church who seem to love to give fervent testimonies about the power of Satan. They say when they try to go to the temple, everything goes wrong. Others say when they go to the temple, their day opens up, all things work better than expected, and they get all green lights. Who is right? Who is God with? The "devil did it" blame game has been with us from the beginning. If you believe Satan has power over your life, work, your car, and the traffic, you are giving the devil a lot of power that he should not and does not really have. With those thoughts, you are empowering satan, literally. But by your knowledge that he does not have any power, you close the door and do not allow him in. We do not resist that evil, as Jesus directed.

119

There is no "darkness" that is more powerful than even the dimmest of the light. What if it was taught that the power of Satan goes near the power of Santa Claus? We do not have to wait to "bind Satan for a season." We can do it now.

5. ...Needing pain, trials, and struggle to grow?

Growth is certainly part of being an eternally evolving being, but do we need to, or should we seek out eating bitter fruit so we can grow? God does not (can't) send trials or tests (James 1:13). Alma addressed this question or principle, and it is not only one of the most profound in all recorded scripture but one of the most powerful ideas pertaining to living the life that you intended when you came here.

"And now, because ye are compelled to be humble blessed are ye; for a man sometimes, if he is compelled to be humble, seeketh repentance; and now surely, whosoever repenteth shall find mercy; and he that findeth mercy and endureth to the end the same shall be saved. ~Alma 32:13

"Therefore, blessed are they who humble themselves without being compelled to be humble." ~Alma 32:16

There appears to be a choice; people can compel themselves or be compelled. To "be compelled" seems to denote an outside force. There is no option not to be compelled. One can be proactive or reactive. The scripture reads, "is compelled to be humble, seeketh repentance..." If one knew their true place in relationship to God, they would be humble. Jesus was the humblest man that has ever walked the earth, and He was no weakling. He had absolute power flowing through him at all times. He knew with certainty who he really was and his place in his relationship with God. He was never boastful or arrogant about it. He knew His true place with God. And the definition of repentance means change. For an eternal being, the change should be constant. It may not always be as drastic as a vice to virtue, but virtue to a little more virtuous; always becoming more like God.

Now, those that are compelling themselves are actively engaged in becoming more like God. They are growing, learning, reading hard books, and having a hard looking at themselves and their life; they are constantly repenting. These do not need to be compelled by life being dragged, kicking, and screaming. Life's fruits are not the function of a moody, angry God sending them to you; they are fruits from the seeds of your mind. If a new house is constructed, the yard is devoid of all plant life. If one does not plant grass and other plants soon, the yard will be filled with a mix of all kinds of plants; some will be wanted but planted in the wrong areas, most will be weeds, and all will be unattractive. This is how many people's lives are lived—a mix of seemingly random fruits, very messy, and a bit chaotic. With no intentions, goals, or discipline of thought, like a ship without a sail and rudder, life will seem very random. They will end up at all kinds of destinations, some wanted and some unwanted. In tasting some of the bitter fruits, they may find themselves asking for "mercy." If they repent or start to direct and change their thoughts, they are changing the seeds for the next season. Changing the seeds will change the fruit, and the new sweet fruit will seem like a merciful God send.

If you do not give up all your sins, you will have to be compelled, which means life is going to beat you up, and it is going to be hard. There will be a struggle; there will be pain; there will be a disappointment. There will be feelings of hopelessness, frustration, depression, anger, and fear until you give up all of those sins (things that disconnect you from God). But if one is actively engaged in a good cause and constantly repenting or changing for the better, they will find that life is not compelling them with bitter fruits at unwanted destinations. And that is how you intended to live.

6. ...Women & The Priesthood

In the early 2010s, momentum, awareness, and publicity increased about LDS women wanting to be ordained to the priesthood. One of their leaders explained, "I've felt the awe of watching my husband exercise his priesthood to bless others and wish that I, too, could pull down the powers of heaven."

This is a perfect example of the "vending-machine-God" sneaking back again, meaning the vending machine will not give the goods unless tokens of prayer with "Priesthood" are stamped on them are put into the machine. Jesus taught "whatsoever ye desire," and the requirements are "believing that ye have received." Meaning finding harmony with one's desire is the path, NOT that a priesthood holder has to offer up the mechanical prayer. Jesus did not teach, "whatsoever ye desire, the condition being offered by someone who has the priesthood, then I may actually feel like getting around to it, otherwise, no." In fact, if a faithful priesthood holder or blessing recipient has a desire yet does not have belief or harmony with it, it cannot come to fruition. No exception.

In Luke 9:49, Jesus's disciples were concerned about seeing others doing miracles or other good acts. "And John answered and said, Master, we saw one casting out devils in thy name; and we forbade him because he followeth not with us." Not only were these men not even members, but they were also not ordained to the priesthood, and yet they were performing miracles. It is never about someone's priesthood status, worthiness, race, religion, or gender. It's about harmony with their desire to be a powerful influencer for good. If it were because of the person's priesthood status, worthiness, or gender that would make God a respecter of persons, a conditional lover, a changeable being, and the laws of the universe would no longer be valid.

Some must view God's "prayer requests" as an in-basket in which they believe God requires a priesthood holding the "Y" chromosome to be attached to formal requests for them to be looked at or really considered. They must view an angel sitting on a cloud saying, "Well, here is a sincere request, if only it had been offered by a man with the priesthood..." And with a quick motion, "DENIED" in red is stamped on the request. God does not operate that way. It is ludicrous even to imagine or entertain such a notion.

I pity the woman (and her family) who feel like they lack power in their life without a "priesthood holder" in their home.

AWAKE and ARISE to your own infinite power. Recognize your absolute connection to God Almighty. If any man (or woman) has ever told you that you are not as powerful as a man with the priesthood, you have been lied to–and that is why it felt bad because God did not agree. You are part of God. You have full, complete, and unlimited access to all that God has and is. There is no membership card you have to swipe to access it. One woman who is connected to God, who is in harmony with her desire, is more powerful than ALL of the priesthood holders in the world who lack harmony with God and their desire.

How do the following two statements feel to you? Which one tugs at your soul's heartstrings with delicious, heavenly, confirming delight? And which one feels off?

-You are a powerful, infinite being, part of God, and you have unlimited power to fulfill all that you desire in this life.

or

-You are a second-class child of God, not as powerful as others. You can still pray and stuff, but if you really want anything done, you should find 1. a male, 2. an LDS male, 3. a faithful, active LDS male, 4. said male who is in harmony with God at the moment, 5. a male who has experience in calling down the powers of heaven, and 6. a male who can ask God for and on behalf of you.

Your heart has spoken the truth to you, and do not let anyone convince you otherwise what inspiration has taught from on high.

7. ...The 10 Commandments & the Doctrine of Supersessionism

The doctrine of supersessionism (or replacement theology or fulfillment theology) answers the question, "Do Jesus's teachings replace (or supersede) the Law of Moses?"

If one does believe in the doctrine of Supersessionism, this means you can no longer quote any of the 613 commandments as doctrine, even if you really, *really* like or agree with some of them.

123

From what I can gather, ancient and modern-day Christians cherry-picked about 75 of them. Nowhere did Jesus reinstate 12.2% or 75 of the 613 commandments. Anyone cherry-picking and quoting ANY of the 613 commandments as God's current viewpoint should be a huge red flag as it's not doctrinal and 100% contrary to what Jesus taught–manipulation is most assuredly afoot.

If one does NOT believe in the doctrine of Supersessionism, this means that we are still under all 613 commandments as doctrine in addition to Jesus's love-centric teachings. This is called Dual-Covenant theology. Personally, I think the New Testament clearly explains the doctrine of Supersessionism:

"Do not think that I have come to abolish the Law or the Prophets; I have not come to abolish them, but to fulfill them. For verily, I say unto you, Till heaven and earth pass, one jot or one tittle shall in no wise pass from the law, till all be fulfilled." ~ Matthew 5:17-18:

The new commandment is just love. God is also love because when you focus your thoughts in a manner in which you receive the indicator of love, that means you are connected to God in that thought and can now be inspired in all things. People seem to like that, but they don't know how that would work in reality.

But if ye be led of the spirit, we are not under the law. ~Galatians 5:18

I personally believe in the doctrine of Supersessionism. Jesus didn't say he was going to fulfill only 87.7% of the Law of Moses. The 613 commandments are made obsolete, and now choices are made by following your love-guided, inspired paths.

Many people do not like "inspiration." It seems shaky, inconsistent, and vague. They'd rather have clear-cut rules and guidelines. It makes them insecure and scared. They also incorrectly think that without the threat of commandments, people will do bad things. So, they cherry-pick some of their favorite Jewish commandments. Picking only your favorite commandments is false doctrine; it's all or none. Meaning, that if you do not believe in the
124

doctrine of supersessionism, you need to be following ALL their commandments as well. For example, this is taken from my other book, Origins - Deeper Truths of Christian Rituals and Doctrines Uncovered by Archaeological Forensics:

"The story follows that the Law of Moses was 613 commandments straight from God. These 613 rules would help govern all humankind in their dealings with their fellow man and their relationship with God. The "10 Commandments" were cherry-picked by Christians; the Jews do not separate those ten out as they are no more or less important than the other 603 commandments. All 613 commandments apply to all men and women on the whole earth, forever. Here are a few commandments from the 613:

- Kill any children you can find from the tribe of Amalek
- Hold eternal grudges (against certain tribes)
- Never offer a peace treaty to certain tribes (Ammonites and the Moabites)
- Kill all Canaanite tribe members from the land of Israel
- Treat your Jewish slaves better than slaves from another tribe (treat the others harshly)
- If you are a priest, thou shalt not eat grape skins, grape seeds, whole grapes, dried grapes (raisins), or grape juice or drink wine made from non-Jews
- Leave single grapes on the vine for the poor, and don't gather grapes that have fallen on the ground
- If you become pregnant from your rapist, you have to marry him and never divorce
- Never go into any building with a dead person in it
- Kings cannot have "too many" horses, gold, or wives
- Thou Shalt not wear garments out of wool and linen mixed
- Thou Shalt not eat fruit of trees for the first three years
- Thou Shalt not plow in a rocky valley
- Provide a city of exile to those who commit manslaughter

- If a man is fighting with another man and if his wife grabs the other's genitals, you must cut off her hand "without hesitation or pity"
- Thou shalt not sell any beautiful virgin women you capture in war. Keep them for yourself (you should murder or sell into slavery the unattractive ones)

Does it feel like those are really eternal, universal, worldwide commandments from an unchanging, unconditionally loving God? Are they being taken out of context? What is the "proper context" for God's prophet ordering the slaughter of innocent children and the capture and personal enslavement of only the prettiest, young virgin girls for themselves?

"Have you allowed all the women to live?" he asked them.
"They were the ones who followed Balaam's advice and enticed the Israelites to be unfaithful to the Lord in the Peor incident so that a plague struck the Lord's people. Now kill all the boys. And kill every woman who has slept with a man, but save for yourselves every girl who has never slept with a man."

~Numbers 31:15-18

You are free to decide for yourself, but I personally do not believe an unchanging, unconditionally loving God would command all people on the planet, including some remote island community halfway around the world, to join in the genocide of a single, feuding, Mediterranean desert tribe in the bronze age who "coincidentally" were their enemies. Was the tribe of Judah questioning, "Who are the children of the tribe of Amalek? Who are the tribes of the Canaanites and Moabites? What did they do to offend God?" or were they like, "Yeah! God told us to kill those jerks our fathers told us to hate! Seeee, it is even a commandment from our God!" Did God really need one tribe to wipe out other tribes? Using no conjecture, using only hard numbers directly out of the text in the Old Testament, God killed over two million people in a

126

vengeful rage. He did not need one tribe to kill other tribe members God did not like.

Their "God" apparently really does not like grapes either. He has SEVEN commandments about grapes. Yet his only thought about rape is: "if you do it and impregnate her, you must marry and never divorce her" rather than: "Thou shalt not rape." Maybe the God of the Old Testament was on the fence trying to decide whether to ban slavery, rape, or bacon. Did He make the right choice? Are these commandments really of God? You can feel the truth. All worldwide communities and religions forbid stealing, murdering, and lying. It makes for a functioning society. Those were not new ideas."

In America, people ignore the higher law to love one another and instead hand-picked Old Testament commandments to justify slavery, abuse of blacks, gays, unwed mothers, minorities, and non-church members. But they ignored all the commandments because they did not agree with them. For example, hunting down and murdering children from certain ethnic groups *seemed* wrong, and so did stoning people or requiring a rape victim to marry their impregnator. You are free to choose for yourself. Again, there is no place where Jesus sorted out which of the 613 commandments should be disregarded and which ones should still be followed; they are either all fulfilled or they are not.

The higher law now is love and then inspiration. People think inspiration means others will just do whatever they feel like; this is not the doctrine. Receiving the indicator of Love (connection to God) is the all-important first step. Once that connection has been established, would someone feel inspired to murder or hurt someone else? I don't think so. So, in a way, they are still actually following Old Testament commandments, but it is internal. It's who they are inside, being guided by God instead of having external, threatening commandments directing them.

Commandments can never be a hard and fast rule; just look at "Thou shalt not kill." What if they are going to kill you? What if they are going to kill another? If there must be exceptions for murder, there must be exceptions for every other commandment as well. That is why commandments will always fall short, and inspired pathways will always triumph...

Which is exactly what Jesus was trying to teach.

The End

For other books, articles, more question and answers visit